I0490480

Network Marketing Made Simple

By

Wale Oyeniyi

Copyright © January 2020 by Wale Oyeniyi

All Rights Reserved. Contents of this book may not be reproduced in any way or by any means without the written consent of the publisher, except for brief excerpts in critical reviews and articles.

Published By:

RightFinder Media

RIGHTFINDER INTERNATIONAL

Website: www.waleoyeniyi.com

Email: info@waleoyeniyi.com

Unless otherwise indicated, all Scripture quotations are taken from the King James Version.

Verses marked NKJV are taken from the New King James Version. Copyright © 1982 by Thomas Nelson, Inc. Used by permission. All rights reserved.

All texts, calls, letters, testimonies, and inquiries are welcome.

Table of Contents

Chapter 1: What Is Network Marketing

Network Marketing also referred to as multi-level marketing (MLM) is a type of marketing strategy, or business model that involves the marketing of products or services by independent representatives, working with a flexible schedule – in most cases from home.

Network Marketing is called many names, including: cellular marketing, consumer direct marketing, multi-level marketing, referral marketing, affiliate marketing and home based business franchising.

How Network Marketing Works

Network Marketing is a type of business where people buy into a company as distributors and they make their money or get a commission by selling the products or services the company has to offer.

This business model is loved by many as it provides them the opportunity to become their own boss, work at their own time and schedule, and dedicate their time and effort in building their own business to the level of success they desire, rather than simply help to build someone else's business.

Network marketing involves a group of people (network) that sell a particular company's products or services. These sellers are called distributors. The distributors recruit or add people to the network, called "downlines."

The distributors make money or get a commission when:

- A product is sold
- When he successfully recruits a down-line
- When a down-line sells a product.

This is basically how network marketing works. When a person X successfully recruits another person Y under them, X will receive a commission from his own sales, and also receives commission from any sales made by Y. In order to make more money and receive higher commission, Y will recruit another person Z under him, and the network goes on and on.

So, the main motivating factor and focus of every member of that network is to recruit more members into the network and to sell more products in order to make more money.

For network marketing companies, profits are earned when they make more sales, grow their business and add new recruits. The company distributes a percentage of its gains to its down-line members in accordance with the compensation plan of the company.

Companies that employ the network marketing model to market their products or services, create different stages and levels of sales representatives to help market their products.

In this model, sales representatives are encouraged, and in most cases motivated, to recruit a network of other salespeople. The salesperson who recruits other salespeople is called an up-line, and receives a percentage or commission from the sales made by the salespeople he recruited (down-line), as well as from his own sales.

Network Marketing is a big business and a noble profession that is taken seriously by people in the First World countries, but unfortunately that is not the case in Africa, because in Africa, people perceive network marketing to a low class type of business/job/career, so they prefer to have a regular job/office work where it is perceived that they will be better respected for what they do.

Network marketing is as old as creation itself, and the Christian faith believes that the creation of man was as a result of networking between God and other heavenly beings. God created other creatures and every other thing on earth, but when it got to the turn of creating man, God extended His reach to the Son and the Holy Spirit. God said, "Let us make man in our image." So no man that lives on the surface of the earth is an island, networking and reaching out to other people widens our horizon and enables us to achieve growth and success.

Networking has become an integral part of life and business to the extent that banks have adopted the networking marketing system as part of their business. Currently, one of the leading banks in the country has deployed a network marketing strategy to get more customers with a message that says "Earn N100 for every new customer you introduce to XXBank. Dial *2019*757# NOW and get your FREE XXBank account to start. No Charges.

What people who doubt the legitimacy, growth potential and the success that can be achieved through network marketing should ask themselves is, if banks as rich as they are and the number of branches they have, could introduce referral system into their business to drive growth and achieve more success, who am I not to use the same method to grow my business and become successful?

The good thing about network marketing, which makes this model of marketing so interesting is that the level created can produce another level, which increases the earning capacity of the salesperson at the top, and even the person in the middle level. So in essence, the commissions that will be earned by salespeople, is totally dependent on the number of people recruited and the volume of product sold. The salespeople who join the business early and dedicate their time and resources into growing stand a better chance of making it to the top and earning more.

The Network Marketing industry is growing and expanding daily with a lot of people keying in and buying into the business model to achieve the financial success and freedom they desire, and escape the inflexible and hectic 9 – 5 working life style.

As a business model, network marketing is very lucrative and a business of choice for anyone who has the desire to grow their own business and achieve financial freedom, but adequate research is needed to choose the right company that offers the right products which can enable you achieve your financial desire.

The main reason network marketing is an ideal, workable business model is that it is open and available to everyone irrespective of status and academic qualification. All you need to succeed and become a millionaire in this business model is your dedication and commitment to succeed.

There are many companies involved in network marketing, but adequate care and proper research need to be done before you settle for a reputable and trusted network marketing company that suits you.

The great thing about network marketing is that if you possess great energy, enthusiasm, have persuasive sales skills, and are willing to persevere, you will build a very rewarding and profitable business with very little capital investment.

So, if you are looking for an opportunity to make additional income, or you want to grow a brand as an entrepreneur, choosing the network marketing option, and leveraging on network marketing platforms as a distributor would be a very good option for you.

Network marketing companies provide their sales distributors with a product, a comprehensive marketing plan, support, mentorship and the necessary trainings to succeed. It is a well packaged business model that gives you all that you need to get started and succeed.

Bear this in mind: network marketing is not a get-rich-quick scheme, and does not guarantee you fast and automatic success. But with diligence, a good marketing plan, the right product and perseverance you will succeed beyond your dreams!

Many new entrants into network marketing make the costly mistake of not taking it as a business venture that has the capacity to grow into something very big and successful, so when a little not-so-good tide comes their way, they chicken out and lose the passion to carry on!

However, if you come into network marketing with the mindset that you are running a business venture, one that has the capacity to change your financial situation, then you will surely succeed.

The fact that network marketing business has a ready-made product, a marketing plan, and the necessary support you need does not mean the business will run itself. You have to run it as a business venture.

Dispelling Network Marketing Myths

A lot of people are either misinformed or ignorant about network marketing, and believe myths about how the network marketing model really works.

Network marketing is not an illegal pyramid system as some misinformed people claim, and you don't need to force people to join your network, or buy your products.

The pyramids here are real and workable, and with a good marketing and sales strategy you will get people to buy your products.

Any member of a network marketing group can become very successful irrespective of where they find themselves in the group, and the myth that the network can become saturated is false and impossible.

Don't make the mistake of letting lies and myths peddled by misinformed and ignorant people cloud your judgment, and deprive you of the opportunity to key into the awesome potential in network marketing.

Things to Consider Before Joining a Network Marketing Platform

It is not a fast and get rich quick scheme, but with adequate work, determination and sales skill, you will become rich through it.

- Check the record of the people that founded the company to know how credible they are. This can be done by checking out their track record in that business model.

- Does the product or service offered by the company appeal to you as an individual? This is very important, because you will be motivated in spending your time and money to market the product.

- What is the promotion model of the company? Can you improve on it if it does not meet up to the standard you like?

- Do you see success coming your way early enough if you dedicate time and finance on this project?

- Do you key into the vision of the company, or are you in only for the financial gain? Keying into the short term and long term vision guarantees your success in this marketing model.

The Prospects In Network Marketing

Network Marketing as a business model involves adaptability, creative way of networking, and being able to generate income for the people that actually work for the networking marketing company. The chances of achieving the desired success you seek is way beyond marketing to your friends and family, and trying to benefit by recruiting them, but it goes beyond that scope by building a group of dedicated people who need the product and are willing to be part of your team.

Network Marketing is highly effective, and if properly done has the potential to become a steady and reliable source of good income. For newbies into network marketing, the model enables them to receive adequate training which helps them become better salespeople, and be able to train others into becoming better network marketers.

In network marketing, the company's distributors gets their income in different ways such as:

- Commissions from the products sold
- Bonus from the performance of your team

- A certain percentage from sales made by members of your team

Network Marketing has become part of our daily life, but we do it every day without getting paid for our efforts and services. I know you are wondering how am I doing network marketing without knowing it. Then check this out.

Have you at any time recommended a certain service or product that you love to a friend, a family member or colleague? If yes, then you are doing network marketing without being paid for it.

Let me ask: were you compensated for recommending that interesting movie you saw recently to every single person in your network of friends? I guess no. Imagine if you could leverage on your network of friends by offering them a value driven product that they cannot resist. This why network marketing is an ideal business of choice for everyone who desires success, because the network you need to grow your business already exists, all you need is to maximize it.

Chapter 2: 27 Reasons Why People Hate Network Marketing

Auto-Ship (Buying Of Products)

Auto-ship is a method that is used in network marketing. It involves the regular shipment of a particular product to a customer at a particular time. It is driven by a standing order, and the payment system is automatic. Auto-ship enables the customer to determine a certain time or schedule that the products will be delivered to them, and it is usually on a regularly basis.

Auto-ship enables a marketing representative to make sure that his level of commission is maintained, and this is done when he meets sales criteria at a certain period, like every 3 months. Auto-ship is one of the ways that network marketers make residual income, and it enables the distributors to use the products from time to time, in order to make informed recommendations to customers.

Some people hate network marketing and consequently run away from it because they consider the auto-ship too expensive, hence they stop it. But you have to bear in mind that there is no good, income generating business you can do effectively without income. Every good business needs income to be invested, but the good thing about network marketing is that the investment needed is small.

A lot of people that opted for auto-ship tend to cancel their auto-ship order and quit network marketing in three months because of the cost involved. Some people prefer to buy the products when they join the company as distributors, and place the order for product when the need arises than signing up for auto-ship.

Referral (The Inability To Get People To Recommend)

Referral marketing is a method of recommending a product or service to friends, family, colleagues and other prospects. Referral happens through word of mouth, that is, one on one marketing to a prospect, holding a seminar to recruit prospects and even positive feedback from other customers that bought your product.

In marketing generally, organic marketing is seldom effective, so referral marketing is an ideal and effective way for a network marketer to make sales and register more prospects. But a lot of people hate network marketing because of this referral method. This is simply because they lack the necessary skills required to convince people to join the networking program.

Anyone who desires success in networking should know that humans are social creatures by nature, and they need recommendation from people they know and trust to subscribe to a product or service.

People make the costly mistake of hating the referral method in network marketing instead of leveraging on this awesome sales and recruitment method to grow their network marketing business. Referral works better than paid adverts and other methods of marketing products and services.

Studies have shown that 83 percent of people that will buy a product or subscribe to a service rely on the advice and recommendation of the people they love and trust, and this is very true because a potential customer has four times more chance of making an order if they receive recommendation from a friend or someone they trust.

It is also believed that 49% of people that order a product or subscribe to a service do so because their friends and family made them aware of the product. This is because, the more satisfied customers talk about your product, the more customers you get. People who hate the referral method of network marketing are either too lazy to do the recommendations involved or misinformed about the potential of referrals.

Delay In Payment

Network marketing is not a get-rich-quick scheme; a lot of hard work, training, mentorship and patience are required to succeed, but once you have gotten the necessary trainings and mastered the skills, you will surely succeed beyond your expectation!

Some people quit network marketing because they hate delay in payment. Delay payment is a sign of a company that does not have a good payment system. This is because if your network marketing company is a serious and legitimate one, they will process your payment promptly and deposit your money into the bank account you provided.

All good network marketing companies have their payment well sorted out to ease payment problems for their distributors. Delay in payments might be a sign of a company going out of business, so be careful and watch if the trend continues for a long time, and if it does, then it might be the time to leave the company.

Postponement Of Payment

Postponement of payment is another reason people give for hating network marketing, and this happens when the company has delayed payment for some time and decide to postpone the payment to a later date.

There are many reasons this could happen: it could be that the company has money problems, or the company has an incompetent financial team, or it is not making profits. All these are red flags, and indicate that the company is not healthy.

Once a company starts experiencing cash flow problems, it would begin postponing the payments of its distributors until it bounces back financially strong and healthy.

If your network marketing company consistently postpones payments, and you don't get satisfactory reasons for that, then you need to be concerned. However, if it only happens for a short time, and you get a good explanation for it, then you have nothing to worry about.

Expensive Products

Some dislike network marketing because, according to them, the products are expensive, and they are unable to afford them.

And this, they say, negatively affects their efforts to recruit more people into the business as many people can't afford the products.

You will agree with me that what determines the value of a product is its quality and efficacy, not size. And so, you should not hate network marketing because of the expensive products. Rather, I would encourage that you develop efficient marketing strategies to sell the product, and persuade prospects to join the business.

The truth is that most people are looking for products that offer maximum value for their money, and are willing to pay for them. And believe me; network marketing products are exactly that - they are good value for your money!

This is what I believe you should focus on if you want to join network marketing business and succeed!

Companies that adopt the network marketing model generally deal in effective, high quality products. This ensures that their customers get full value for their money when they buy the products.

These companies also understand that their products are the lifeblood of the business, and because some go as far as offering customers a 30-day guarantee on the products they buy, because they trust the quality of their products. This is something you won't find in conventional retail outlets.

Lack of Automation

Automation, lead generation, online marketing funnels and traffic are the latest and the most effective methods and tools that drive both sales and recruitment in network marketing.

But at the start, there is no automation. Everything is done in person. Your prospecting, training, and enrolling prospects into the business, all these are done manually. You do them yourself when you first join the business.

And unfortunately, this is one aspect some do not like about network marketing.

You need to understand that at the beginning, what you should focus on is to learn the skills that will make you an effective network marketer, which include:

- Doing One-On-One Presentations,
- One-On-One Recruiting Of Prospects,
- One-On-One Trainings,
- Group Presentations And Seminars

What this implies that your performance and success is entirely up to you. Many run away from network marketing because of this.

Over time, however, it actually gets better. In time, you can automate your network marketing, generate more leads and grow your business.

Automation actually means to set up a system that helps you to get new prospects to enroll, and help you sell your product digitally. With an effective automation system in place, you may not need to constantly try to convince friends, family members, colleagues and any prospects you meet.

A good example of digitally automating your network marketing business for effective growth is through Facebook ads, which you can use to target your prospective audience.

Matrix Compensation Plan

Another aspect of network marketing some do not like is the Matrix Compensation Plan. This is a type of pyramid structure arranged in rows (width) and columns (depth). It is a structure that limits the number of people (distributors) you are eligible to sponsor if you are at the first level.

In network marketing, distributors make money through profits and bonuses. They buy products at wholesale and resell (retail) for a profit, and earn bonuses from down-line sales.

Of all the compensation plans, the matrix compensation plan seems the most effective, but some still do not like it because of the work involved. Here, you need to fill up your distributors in the frontline, before you can build under any other person.

If you recruit say two people, you can put them under one another, and they can build the group together. But a problem can occur if a distributor opts out. If that distributor has not sponsored anybody, then you have to build again; but if the distributor has sponsored others before, the departure creates a hole in the matrix, that is impossible to fill. In this position you will never receive your payment. This is one of the things that some people hate about network marketing.

In the matrix compensation plan, the forced matrix system actually limits the depth of your payment. Maximizing a matrix compensation plan is the key to success, because things can look perfect at first, but then can go wrong if the plan is wrongly designed.

Another thing that makes some not like network marketing, and especially the matrix compensation plan is that it is a little difficult to explain. This is because they find it hard to fully understand the structure of the compensation plan, and as well as the variation in payment scale.

To reduce the chances of failure, it is important to seek out a simple compensation plan; this will help eliminate potential problems that could rise if a distributor opts out.

The matrix compensation plan has its advantages, however, which any hardworking, driven and determined network marketer can leverage on to achieve success.

Among these advantages are:

Matrix compensation plan enables direct sellers to remain coordinated, making it very easy for them to attract and recruit new distributors. This ease is enabled by the width and depth of the structure.

The plan also motivates the team members to work together since everyone makes a profit and get benefits.

The most interesting thing about matrix compensation plan is that once you are able to fill associates/distributors in the frontline, then your focus will be on making the associates/distributors in your frontline into leaders. You teach and motivate to achieve this.

It is used to encourage them which in turn multiply your success.

Selling Of Products (Hawking)

Some see the selling of products involved in network marketing as "hawking", and do not like the model because of this. To these people, selling products is below their status, they see it as something degrading.

The real problem, however, is not that these people don't like selling, but their fear of rejection. They fear being rejected when they try to market a product to someone, or try to recruit prospect.

Also, in Africa, people still look down on hawkers and marketers, while many still consider network marketing a low-class business/career. They prefer the prestige that comes with working in a corporate office where they are under-valued and under-paid, rather than "get their hands dirty" reaching out to prospective customers to market their product and making some good money.

Unlike in First World countries where network marketing is as seen as a serious career and business, many Africans still do not see network marketing as a business that you can build your career upon or totally rely on as a stable means of income. This notion is however founded on ignorance and misinformation.

As in any field of endeavor, information, that is, the right information is key. The facts that back network marketing as a viable business cannot be denied. Figures show that network marketing has produced the highest paid professionals and has made more millionaires than any other industry.

To set the record straight, there is more to network marketing than simply hawking products. It is a business, and a lucrative one at that, which can make you financially free, and live the life of your dreams. So I encourage you to do your research and learn how network marketing really works, and possibly get someone to mentor you before you decide if network marketing is for you or not.

Time Factor For Distributor

One of the reasons people also give for hating network marketing is the length of time it takes to market products and convince new prospects to join the business.

Network marketing is a business, and like any traditional business, it requires time and dedication to succeed. So, if you desire to succeed at it, you must give it the time and dedication it needs.

The truth is that if you cannot dedicate time to the success of your network marketing business, then you shouldn't be in the business at all.

A lot of people erroneously think that network marketing is a part-time business, one that you only need to invest little time into and see it grow and succeed. But that's not the case. The worse part about this is that people join the business with this belief, only to get in and discover they were lied to.

Time, effort and dedication are the foundation of success in any business. And if you come into network marketing with the mindset that you are in a business, you will put in the work required to make it profitable for you.

A lot of people join network marketing based on the success stories that they see and hear, but the truth is that those who succeed in network marketing dedicate their time and effort to achieve success. So, if you desire to replicate their success, you must be ready to dedicate your time to see your network marketing business succeed.

Difficulty In Selling Products

Another reason many give for hating network marketing is the difficulty in selling products. But this is neither the fault of network marketing as a business, nor of the product being marketed; this is simply because the people involved do not take adequate time to master the skill of selling, which demands that you study the target audience and present the products to them in an irresistible manner.

Marketing is an act, and it requires patience, dedication and repeated practice to master. And once you master it, you can sell anything to anyone!

Products by network marketing companies sell are high quality, effective, value-driven and well-packaged. So, if there is difficulty in selling it, it is not because of the product, but the inability of the seller. The truth is, to be a good salesperson you need to be in love with the act of selling. This is because if you lack the needed passion as a salesperson, you will fail irrespective of how good the product you are selling is!

A lot of people find it difficult to sell because of the fear of rejection, but you need to know that rejection is part of the trade. It is not a question of whether you will face rejection, what really matter is how you respond to it. Do you chicken out, or do you repackage yourself with renewed energy, drive and motivation to close the next sale? I strongly encourage you to choose the latter.

One thing you must understand when it comes to selling is that people don't like to part with their part with their money. And if you're not willing to face rejection and still keep pushing, then the truth is network marketing is not for you!

You must formulate an effective selling strategy, with a relevant and strong value proposition, and patiently convince your potential buyers before they can buy from you.

Attitude (Insincerity) Of Uplines/Sponsors

Up-line and down-line are two types of compensation structures that determines where a particular person belongs and the roles they play in the structure.

An up-line is a term used in referring to the person that brought you into the network marketing company. That person is called your sponsor/up-line. Others who are above you are also your up-lines. Your up-lines gets a percentage from the sales you make.

A down-line refers to the new members recruited by those already in the business.

For a good network marketing system to function effectively and bring success to its members, the up-lines and down-lines need to have a good and harmonious working relationship. The up-lines are responsible for training and helping their down-lines understand the business and help them succeed.

But the arrogance and insincerity of some up-lines make new recruits hate the business model and even give up on the business.

An up-line who is only interested in how much money he can make from his down-lines discourages the down-lines, and make them dislike the business.

There is no new recruit in network marketing who will be happy to be under an arrogant, greedy and selfish sponsor. A sponsor who doesn't carry others along, who doesn't care about their welfare and success, or someone who assumes the position of a boss without taking care of the responsibility of leadership.

The sponsor needs to be a leader indeed, who leads his group with honesty, humility, and treats every member of the group with respect. The success of the down-line, to an extent, depends on the attitude and sincerity of the sponsor, since the sponsor plays a major role in helping the down-line build confidence, learn the skills needed to market the products, inspire them to overcome the initial obstacles they might face and give them a roadmap to success.

But if a new recruit joins a network with a leader who lacks these qualities, they will leave the business with a bad experience and hate it as a result.

My advice to anyone that is new to network marketing is to go for a sponsor that is a good leader, mentor, servant, helper and friend. With these qualities in your sponsor, you will surely succeed in network marketing.

Inconsistent Policy Of The Company's Registration/Product Prices

Strong and consistent company policy, well regulated and stable product prices are the bedrock of the strength and growth of a company, and network marketing business is not an exception.

However, when this policy is inconsistent, then the company's network marketers will suffer some loss of money and time. And this is another reason why some hate network marketing.

The policy a network marketing company adopts and its implementation affects how its network marketers perform. If the policy is right and well implemented, it will lead to the growth and success of both the company and its marketers, but if the reverse is the case, it will lead to the failure of the company, and scare away network marketers!

Product prices is another factor that can scare away new entrants into network marketing, and even make the ones already enrolled to back out.

A lot of network marketers complain of lack of sales because the products are expensive. And if the prices keep changing, it becomes very hard to find customers to buy, which makes marketers abandon the business.

Rejection Of Offers (Proposals)

Anyone that intends to succeed and live a financially free life through network marketing should understand that rejection of offer (proposal) is part of the business.

Rejection of offer can leave many people frustrated and discouraged and thus hate network marketing. But this should not be the case, because everyone has experienced one form of rejection or the other, even the multi-million earners in the business.

Rejection should not make you give up on network marketing; rather you should repackage your offer and try again.

The truth is that if you are not mentally strong and prepared to face rejection, and don't develop the determination needed as a salesperson, your feelings will always be hurt by the rejection and lead you to hating network marketing.

If you are scared or worried that your offer might be rejected, then I suggest you start your marketing with the people you know very well, like friends and family, colleagues at work and church members, from there you can grow in confidence and venture into something bigger.

There is a saying I like about sales and the fear of rejection, it goes thus, "rejection doesn't cause disappointment, what you do after the rejection is what brings you disappointment."

The following are ways you can handle rejection:

Focus On What You Can Control.

Your main focus should not be on getting your prospect to immediately say yes to your proposals, rather, you should focus on how to package and present your product that your customer will see its value, or your prospect will see the opportunity in your offer. Don't overpush it because you are not in control of who wants to buy or accept your offer.

But you have the capacity to control:

- Who you want to show
- The time you want to show
- The way you show

- What you show
- Where you chose to show

Handle Your Rejection Positively

The best way to handle rejection is to be positive about it. Don't take it personally, or take it as a sign that you will fail in the business that you find yourself, don't let it affect your confidence and don't quit.

That someone rejected your offer doesn't mean the person rejected you as a person. They just said "NO" to your product or offer, but they might be in need of it tomorrow and say "YES" so never take it personal.

Societal Factor – Belief, Scam And Deceit

Due to ignorance and misinformation, a lot of people believe network marketing is nothing but a scam, a way to collect money from gullible people in the society.

This mindset has made a lot of people to hate network marketing, and consequently, miss out on the opportunities in this lucrative business model.

To really help us know that network marketing is not a scam, or just a means to dupe people, we need to first understand what network marketing is not.

Network marketing is not a pyramid scheme. A pyramid scheme or program is one where you are promised that if you invest a certain amount of money, in time you will get great returns and become very rich. A pyramid scheme is not commerce or business oriented, it doesn't have a product to sell or a service to offer, it is just a money doubling scheme. Though some fraudulent pyramid scheme might present a product to sell, it is only a disguise for the money doubling scheme.

Network marketing, on its part, is a legitimate and registered business with products and services that solve genuine problems in the society.

People who make a lot of money in network marketing do so, not by scamming others, but through the dedication of their time and money to build a network that provides value to people, and sell problem solving products.

Pyramid schemes are what those who hate network marketing actually hates without taking the time to understand the difference the two models. In a pyramid scheme someone has to lose their hard earned money before someone else can make money, whereas in network marketing each member of the network can multiply their earnings if they put more efforts in helping other people in the network to succeed.

Though there has been cases of people being scammed or duped in the name of network marketing by greedy and fraudulent individuals, but that doesn't mean that network marketing as a business model is a scam.

The network marketing model is not designed to scam people, but to provide products and services to the people that actually need them. Therefore, believing that network marketing is scam and hating it because of that is not the way forward. Do a proper research, and choose a networking company that has years of proven integrity and enroll with someone you trust.

Misconception – Thinking It Is A Get Rich Quick Scheme

Some people come into network marketing thinking it is a get rich quick scheme, but they become very disappointed when they come into the business and find out that it is nothing like that.

The truth is that network marketing is NOT a get-rich-quick scheme. But like many other legitimate businesses, if you invest the required hard work, determination, passion, with patience and mentorship, it can make you rich and financially free.

People, who hate network marketing and quit easily when they join, do so because they thought that network marketing is a get rich quick scheme.

It is wrong to come into a genuine, value driven and lucrative business like network marketing with a greedy mindset of making it quick. This mindset is the reason a lot of people fall to pyramid schemes which promise to make them millionaires in three months, and by the time they find out that they have been conned, it would be too late.

A lot of people have become very rich through network marketing, but these success stories didn't happen overnight; many of them have one tale of failure or the other, but they persevered and to build a successful business.

I am not saying that you should not come into network marketing with dreams and expectations, but having an achievable and workable expectation is the key. When coming into network marketing, come with passion and determination to succeed, work hard and expect a good compensation. Also, choose the right network marketing company with value driven products that solve problems, receive the right training and support from your sponsor, but don't come with the mindset of getting rich quick, because all your expectations will end in disappointment. But if you persevere and with the right mindset, you will surely become rich through network marketing.

Return On Investment

Just like any business that requires investment, network marketing requires some level of investment too. But the good part is that the investment required in network marketing is not as much as many other businesses.

But some people are impatient and lack the working knowledge of how network marketing works, thus, when they invest a little money into the business, they want to get their money back as soon as possible. And when this doesn't happen, they consider network marketing a failure, making them to hate it.

Return on investment in network marketing is not predictable. The returns on investment you get depend on how dedicated you are to the business. It depends on the quality of time and effort you put into it to make it successful, so if you are not getting the return on your investment as you expect, it is largely your fault, and not anybody else or even the business.

Network marketing is the ideal business for anyone that is ready and willing to invest time and effort, and little capital to achieve good return on investment.

The ideal way to project return on investment is to have a comprehensive two to five year business plan. It implies that, if you learn the necessary skills needed to succeed, give it your best shot in both time and effort, stay determined and focused, then you can get a return on investment of six figures or even more annually.

Network marketing works differently from conventional business models, in the sense that if your income is lesser than the capital you invest, the business will fail.

This is not how network marketing works, however. Here, the business will fail if you don't give it enough time and effort, and worse, if you are focused on the wrong activities.

The implication of this is that even if you put all the money in the world into network marketing, and you don't give it the needed time and effort, you will never reap your expected return on investment!

So you will hate network marketing if you are predicting how quick you will get your return on investment based on the amount of money you invested. Time, effort and focus drive your return on investment in network marketing.

Startup Capital

The startup capital needed for network marketing business is company specific, that is, the startup capital needed to start with company A is different from that needed to start with company

B. But some people complain that the cost required to start a network marketing business is one of the reasons they hate the business model.

The truth is that, those who complain about the cost of starting a network marketing business have not compared it with that of starting a traditional business. The cost of starting a network marketing business is small, and the good thing about it is that you get the company's products in return, plus starter kits, brochures, training and all the support you need. This is something you will never get in the traditional business model.

In starting a traditional business, you will need money to buy the products, get an office space, set some money aside for running cost and overhead, for staff maintenance and utility bills. Unlike network marketing, where the company provides you with all the necessary support that you need, and you are fully in business.

Like I mentioned earlier, the startup cost needed to start a networking business varies from one company to another, so choose the one you can afford and you are good to go. Out of all the businesses you can do from home, which has the capacity to grow very big, and make you financially free, network marketing requires the least startup cost.

Lack Of Orientation And Education

Most misconception that people have about network marketing is as a result of lack of orientation and proper education about how it works and its abundant possibilities. The people who are ignorant and lack proper tutelage about network marketing are the ones that spread negative stories about this lucrative business model, and make people hate it.

The key factors that determine success in any business are: proper orientation and mentorship, and network marketing is not an exception in this area. So, rather than complain about the model, take time to properly get acquainted with how it works; research and read brochures on the business and look for a mentor to hold your hand and guide you, and you will be glad you did.

A lot of people who have failed in network marketing failed not network marketing is a bad business, but because of the bandwagon effect. They joined thinking it is a get rich quick scheme, without taking time to get the proper orientation and learn the skills needed to succeed. And when things don't go the way they plan, they hate network marketing and convince other ignorant people to do same.

One mistake some new entrants into the business make is that they don't take network marketing as they would a traditional business. And do not develop the skills needed to run a successful business.

If you want to go into the business of selling fabrics, for example, you take the time to learn all the necessary details about the business, and in some cases you may pay for that specialized knowledge, but if you want to go into network marketing business, you pay for the kits and you proceed with your marketing and recruiting new prospects, and you expect it to work effectively and lead to the success you desire? No Way!

You need to acquire the necessary education about network marketing, get someone to mentor you, and the success you desire will come. Lastly, don't let the desire to make quick money be the only reason you go into this business, because you might be disappointed.

Lack Of Awareness Of The Company And Its Products

The ability to do proper research and become fully aware of the network marketing company you want to join, and the types of products they market, is one of the factors that can lead to success if properly done, or result in a big failure if done poorly or not done at all before starting the business.

This is one of the mistakes those who have failed in network marketing made that made them hate the business. They lack the basic knowledge about how the company operates, and how the products work.

Knowledge is the key to success in anything we do in life and any business venture we want to embark on, and without those basic knowledge about the business, failure is sure.

So, if you want to join the business, make sure you research the company you intend to join, and how value driven their products are, better still, you can get a mentor already working with the company they intend to join to educate properly about the company and its products.

One of the best decisions you can make if you're joining the business is to choose a networking marketing company that offers products which you can easily key in to its values, and market effectively.

For a new a new entrant into network marketing that lacks the knowledge about a company and its products, below are some basic tips to help you know the type of company and products to go for:

How Old Is The Company?

One of the most important things to know before joining a network marketing company is, how old that company is and how long they have been operating as a legal and genuine company?

This knowledge is very important, because new companies might not have a good and credible record you can completely rely on, and the tendency of a new company having problems is higher compared to older companies.

The People In The Company

Another important factor to know before choosing a network marketing company is the people that are already involved with the company. This is because your sponsor determines the level of success you will achieve in that company.

Your sponsor will train you, and equip you with the necessary skills you need to succeed. So before joining the company, find out if the people there are trustworthy and reliable. Looj out for people who can go to any length to make sure you succeed, and not those who are exploitative and are only after their own selfish interest.

You also need to be aware that companies tend to attract some certain people according to their concept, so try to attend some meetings and seminars organized by your company of choice before you finally enroll with them. But when you are in such a meeting, carefully look around you to know the type of people that the company attracts, and then decide if it is the type of people you want to do business with.

The Product

The types of products marketed by the company is another very important thing you have to be very knowledgeable about. The quality and value of the products is one of the hallmarks of a good network marketing company.

Network marketing companies offer different types of products such as health and wellness products, beauty and skin care products, household products, personal care products and others. It's important to know the one to go for.

The key is in choosing consumable products that add value to life. The type of products that are in constant demand, and which subscribers buy all the time, not seasonal products, or the products that takes years for customers to buy again.

For example, a health and wellness product is bought every time irrespective of time and season, while some household products like a blender takes years to be replaced.

So, not knowing a company and its products should not be why you hate network marketing. Instead, acquaint yourself with the products offered by a company, and choosing the right products to market will increase your level of success in network marketing.

Myths that first timers are the only people that benefit in network marketing

It is a misconception that the only people that succeed are those who joined the company early enough; and it is born out of ignorance about how network marketing works.

This baseless myth has driven a lot of people from network marketing, and made some to hate this lucrative business model that has the capacity to change their financial destiny and enable them to live a life of financial freedom.

The success in network marketing is not a function of when you join, or how early you join. What actually determines your success is the determination to succeed, your willingness to learn the necessary skills required to succeed, the type of sponsor you have, and the time and effort you put in marketing your products and recruiting new prospects.

In fact, the best time to join a network marketing company is now. Stop procrastinating, get rid of the fear of the unknown, do away with the hate, forget the rumors, lies and misinformation that people who lack knowledge about network marketing are spreading and embrace this lucrative and time tested business model, and you will be glad you did.

Humans are creatures with wants and needs, so the demand for products and service is constantly on the increase. Network marketing is one of the ways through which the wants and needs of people are met, and this is because of the value driven products that network marketing companies provide. So there is no lateness to network marketing, come on board now, and be part of the men and women making so much money and changing lives through network marketing.

Sometimes, (Multi-Level Marketing) MLM Company Fizzle Out

The fear that a network marketing company might fizzle out with time is another reason that some people give for hating network marketing.

While it is true that some marketing companies have fizzled out with time, there are still a lot that have stood the test of time, and still growing stronger and bigger. That is why adequate care and research should be done before joining a network marketing company. Avoid the band wagon effect as much as possible, and seek out seasoned network marketers who have been in a company for a long time and enroll with them.

Let us take a critical look at some of the things that can make a network marketing company to fail and fizzle out in order to enable new entrants into network marketing to avoid them and make informed choices about the company they chose.

Greed

Greed is one of the reasons that have made some network marketing companies to fail and fizzle out. This problem of greed happens when the network marketing company operates a compensation plan which makes it benefit more from the company's profit at the detriment of its distributors.

The mistake their owners made was not appreciating the fact that well-paid and motivated distributors are the bedrock of their business, and when the distributors leave because of poor motivation and compensation, the company will surely fail and fizzle out.

So don't hate network marketing because of fear that the company might fizzle out, but rather look out for and join a company that has a strong track record of motivating their distributors with the needed incentives to grow, and pays them a good compensation plan. The tendency of such companies fizzling out is minimal.

Products.

Network marketing companies that have products that are not value driven, and products that can easily be gotten from any retail store and at a much affordable price have a great tendency to fail and fizzle out. You should watch for such companies and avoid them no matter the mouth-watering offer they come up with.

Look out for companies that their products are solution driven, with high quality assurance, and have no bad and negative reviews, and have been in the market for some time and enroll with such companies.

High Price Of Products And Fake Claims

Some companies offer products that their prices are too high for the average person. This leads to very low patronage, and if the distributors are unable to market the products because of the high price, they get discouraged and leave the marketing company; this in turn can make the company fizzle out.

Another reason that can make a company to fail and fizzle out is fake claims and lies about the efficacy of their products. Some network marketing companies put out unfounded claims that their products can cure any disease and ailment, but when the final consumers buy the products and discover after use that those claims were false, such companies will be flooded with bad and negative reviews which might result in the company fizzling out.

Leaders/Up-Lines And Sponsors Cross Carpeting

There is this negative trend in network marketing that makes some new entrants in the business to hate it, get discouraged and quit the business. This is the tendency of leaders/up-lines joining another company they find more rewarding without taking the adequate time to focus and build their business.

Business growth and success is not something that you can achieve overnight; it requires skills, time, effort, determination and complete dedication to that business. But when the leaders in a network or team of network marketers leave to join another network marketing company, or another business entirely due to personal interest or greed, the whole network might get distorted and fail.

So, it is advisable for new entrants and beginners to enroll under a credible and trusted sponsor that has spent many years in a particular network marketing company, and has a proven track record of success with that company. This will eliminate the failure of leadership due to cross carpeting of leaders/uplines and sponsors.

Working Hard Without Results

Some people complain that the reason they hate network marketing is because they worked hard, but they didn't get a commensurate result for their efforts.

While this reason for hating network marketing might look justifiable and even painful, however, it is not true that network marketing as a business model does not reward people for their efforts or that the people that work hard does not see the result of their efforts.

The real question here is, how knowledgeable are you about network marketing? What skills do you have to drive the growth and success of your business? What network marketing company are you partnering with? And what types of products does it offer?

The answer to these questions will determine if you are working hard in the right direction, or if you are working hard in the wrong direction that will produce no results. Some of the factors that will guarantee that your hard-work in network marketing will produce the desired results are:

The Network Marketing Company You Belong

This is very important because if you belong to a network marketing company that provides the necessary starter kits, the needed training and motivation, and the right compensation plan, you will surely be guaranteed results for your hard work. So, choose the company that you want to partner with wisely.

Knowledge

Knowledge is the key to success in all endeavor and business, and network marketing business is not an exception. If you put all the hard work in this world without the adequate knowledge to succeed in this business model, you will never see any meaningful result. So, acquire the needed knowledge by going for trainings, seminars and relying on your sponsor to teach you the skills needed to succeed and your hard work will start yielding results.

The Right Products

Network marketing is about marketing and selling of products or services. Therefore, if you want your hard work to yield results, you have to choose a network marketing company that has the right products, products that have good value and solve problems.

Only The Influential Succeed

There is a wrong and defeatist reason that some people give for hating network marketing, and that is it is only influential people who succeed in this business.

By influential, they mean people who have a great network of friends and followers like celebrities and those that are rich.

This mindset is wrong and defeatist, because success in any business, including network marketing, a function of hard work, dedication, determination and the right mindset. A lot of successful people in this world and the ones that become rich through network marketing were poor and unknown men and women who believed in their ability to succeed and broke down all the barriers of social status, gender, color, economic and other obstacles to succeed.

Don't be deceived or be limited by your social and economic status because impossible is nothing. The moment you set your heart to a given goal and you are determined to achieve it, nothing can stop you from attaining it. Success is all about your mindset, when your mind is set to a specific goal, you develop, you grow and success embraces you.

If you want to succeed in network marketing, you have to forget the lie that only influential people succeed and start applying the rudiments needed to succeed and you will surely succeed.

When you have the means you can pay for others

Success in network marketing is a function of how big your network is, that is the number of your down-lines. Because of this, some network marketers who have the capacity, pay for others to come into their network.

While this method is a good method to expand your network, it is not enough reason for people to hate network marketing, but some people hate this business opportunity for the sole reason that they don't have the means to pay for others.

In as much as it is a proven fact that network marketing is a very lucrative business that has the capacity to make you rich and achieve financial freedom, the success that you will achieve is not dependent only on how much money you have in your bank account and how many people you can pay for or sponsor, it is about how dedicated you are.

Network marketing was designed in such a way that you don't need a lot of capital and inventory to start and succeed, so there is no reason to hate it because you don't have the means to pay for others, just start with what you have and from where you are right now, and gradually, but consistently grow your business to the level you desire.

Nigeria Government Policy (Weak Regulatory Authority)

Nigeria as a country is riddled with inconsistent and unfriendly policies and weak regulatory authority that hinder the growth and success of businesses.

Unfriendly government policies and weak regulatory authorities are part of the reasons some hate network marketing and quitting the business. Granted, their reason is true and a well-established fact, it should not be a reason not to be part of this lucrative business model.

Despite the harsh economic situation in the country, and the unfriendly government policies, affecting the growth of business, men and woman with the right mindset and determination to succeed are still venturing into the business of their dreams and achieving great success.

There is no right and special time to become a part of the successful family of network marketers, but the best time for you is now.

Know that no venture no success, and if you are waiting for the government policy in Nigeria to get better before you venture into any business of your choice, or the regulatory authorities to become professionals in the conduct of their affairs, then you have set yourself up to become poor and live a life of regrets.

But if your aim is to succeed in any business venture and even in network marketing, then you have to turn those obstacles into stepping stones that will motivate and elevate you to the level of success you desire.

Success has a sweet and lovely address, but the road to that address is not sweet and lovely, it is riddled with obstacles, human and physical barriers that will come against you and try to prevent you from reaching that address and becoming a proud resident of that address, but with dedication, determination and persistent you will overcome all of them and reach it successfully.

Problem Reaching The Right Target Audience

New entrants into network marketing are told by deceitful network marketers that all they need to succeed in this business model is to enroll, get your products and share it amongst your family, friends and colleagues. That means sharing it within your close network.

So the enthusiasm for the business dies and hatred for this business model sets in after they have shared the products among their close network and still not succeeds.

The truth is that your close network alone can't guarantee the growth and success of your business. Yes, it is good to start from there in order to build the needed confidence to reach out and target the right audience that needs the products or services you offer.

So, if you have tried network marketing and failed or you intend to become a part of the successful network marketing family, but you are worried about the problem of reaching the right target audience to showcase your products and services, your worry is a legitimate one that has a solution, but not a reason to hate network marketing.

With the aid of technology like Facebook, Instagram, Google ads and other social media platforms, the marketing of goods and services and the problem of reaching the right target audience that needs your product is now a thing of the past.

For instance, Facebook has a marketing tool called Facebook Audience Insight found in the Facebook Ads Manager that you can use to target the right audience who need your products. With this marketing tool, you can target the right audience using the age, gender, location, their specific needs, their likes and other behavioral patterns to enable you to market your products to the right audience that actually needs them.

So stop worrying and hating network marketing as a business because you lack the right audience to market to, and take advantage of the many marketing and social media platforms to grow your business and achieve the success you desire.

Chapter 3: The Rules That Guarantee Success For A Network Marketer

There Is A Price To Pay

Network marketing like every other business that has the capacity to make you financially independent comes with a price to pay in order to achieve the success you desire, and that price includes:

Investing Time And Money

For you to succeed in network marketing, you need to invest in yourself. Don't have the mentality of trying to get something for nothing. Rather invest in coaching courses, the necessary tools and skills you need to succeed, mentoring, and anything you know will help you run your business successfully.

Be Humble

This is very important because you need humility to learn, follow instructions, and have an open mind to receive constructive criticism that will help you to grow. Network marketing thrive on replication, so you need to have the right mentor that you can replicate their success, and when you have learnt very well you also can mentor others that will be part of your down-lines, but you need humility to learn properly.

Time And Effort

No business will grow and succeed if adequate time and effort is not dedicated to make it work effectively. For network marketing, the level of success you will enjoy and how fast it will happen is a function of the time and effort you put into the business. So in essence, network marketing is not for lazy people, people who are not ready and willing to put in the time and effort needed to succeed, but for people who are ready to give it all it takes.

Have Positive And Right Expectation

People that are not ready to pay the price of success in network marketing, make the big mistake of coming into the business with the mindset that they will become rich in a very short time. They can be disappointed when they discover that it doesn't work that way.

Yes, you can make big money from network marketing, but you need to put in the hard work that comes with it. So, having a positive and right expectation means that you should be objective, and willing to pay the price in acquiring skill, efforts, time and other resources needed to succeed.

The Right Attitude

Attitude is very essential in succeeding in network marketing. You need to know that network marketing is a business. So, if you come in with the attitude that it is a part time job, or a hobby where you can put in little time and effort, and achieve success, then you have programmed yourself to fail.

Do not be deceived by claims that you can succeed and get rich in network marketing when you put in very little time and effort, it is a fallacy! It requires hard work, time and consistent effort to achieve success. Growth and momentum in network marketing is achieved with time, so apply the right attitude every day to grow your business, remain consistent and determined in the face of pressure and obstacles, and you will achieve the success you desire.

There Is Time To Give

Network marketing is a very rewarding and lucrative business, but it is not a get rich quick scheme, it requires time to achieve the desired success.

Time they say is money, and for any network marketer to succeed, they have to put their time into productive activities that will help their business grow.

The concept of working for yourself and at your own time is a concept that many new entrants into network marketing and the ones that failed in this line of business misinterpret to mean you work leisurely at your own pace and at any time you please. This is nothing but a recipe for disaster.

The truth is that, for a new entrant into network marketing and for anyone that desires success in this business, you have to give it enough time to help it grow and become very functional. You need to be disciplined with time and appointments. Don't lose a sale or miss recruiting a new prospect because you couldn't meet up with appointments at the scheduled time.

You only get what you put in into network marketing business. So if you put in enough time to see your business grow, you will reap the benefits, but if you are lazy and neglect to dedicate the time required, then you are guaranteed to fail.

Don't ever make the mistake of joining a network marketing company if you are only after the big money you will make, but don't have time to do the work involved, it will be a waste of time, effort and money, because every business requires time and effort to make it grow, and network marketing is not an exception.

There Is Patience To Exercise

There is a popular saying that, "Patience is a virtue that only the wise possess." This saying holds true and strong in network marketing more than in any other business model.

Lack of patience due to high and unrealistic expectations is one of the reasons a lot of people have either failed or quit midway.

Like I have said so many times in this book, and I will say it once again, "Network marketing is not a get rich quick scheme," but it has the potential to make you rich and financially independent if you are patient enough to learn the necessary skills, patient enough to do the work required and patient enough to grow your business into a big organization.

So, there is nothing like overnight success in network marketing, or cutting corners due to impatience. If any network marketing company promises you overnight success and gets rich without doing much work, then you have to be very careful, because you might become a victim of scam. Your diligence and hard-work is what will distinguish you in network marketing and produce the success your desire.

There are some people who have the notion that network marketing is all about enrolling with a good company, talk to a few people to enroll under them, and the money will flood in and they will become rich. The people that have this unfounded notion are the same people that jump from one network marketing company to another looking for easy and cheap success, they never exercise enough patience to stick with one network marketing company and learn what it takes to succeed.

The success stories that you see and hear about people that made it big in network marketing are about people that were patient enough to build their business from the scratch, passed through one form of obstacle or the other, but they persevered, stayed patient and made it in network marketing.

The people you see, hear or read about their success were patient to build a good reputation, generate great followership, prospects and marketing list, building the necessary skills needed to succeed, developing relationships and investing time and money. All these took them time to achieve, and you too can achieve the level of success they enjoy now if you exercise the same patience they applied.

See your waiting time as a season of sowing, knowing that you will reap the harvest of what you sow, and the more your sowing time, the better and greater the harvest will be. So if you want to become rich through network marketing be patient, build credibility, build a list of dedicated followers and customers, dedicate the needed time and effort, learn and implement the techniques and skills you learn from your sponsor, and success will surely come.

There Is A Seed To Sow

Good and sustainable success in any business venture doesn't come easy and cheap, and network marketing is one of those businesses that can guarantee you financial freedom, so success here to come with a price.

Just like the seed time and harvest that the bible talks about, and the planting and sowing of seeds that produces the harvest of fruits and foods that we love to enjoy, network marketing requires the sowing of seed to succeed.

The seed we need to sow in network marketing to qualify for abundant harvest of success includes the money needed to enroll and obtain the starter kits, products, manuals, brochures and every other thing that the company gives you to help you succeed.

The good thing about network marketing is that the seed money needed to start up is very small compared to other businesses (like we talked about), and once you invest this seed money, the company will set you up to succeed by giving you all the necessary materials you need to succeed. There is also the seed of time and effort to sow in order to succeed, the seed of knowledge to be acquired, and the seed of investing in seminars, books, CDs and other materials that you need to succeed.

The amazing thing is that these seeds are not too expensive, but the harvest and gains are big and life changing. Therefore, if you desire to achieve success in your network marketing venture, sow the necessary seeds and success will surely come.

There Is Education To Acquire

The popular saying that, "knowledge is Power" is so true in network marketing.

Success in network marketing is not too difficult. In fact, it is easier than the traditional business model if you dedicate the time needed to acquire the basic education and knowledge needed to succeed.

Let us take a look at some of the skills you need to acquire in order to succeed in network marketing:

The Skill Of Networking

The power of networking is one of the most important skills you need to acquire in order to achieve success in network marketing. The strength of your network determines the level of success you will achieve. So you need to get fully educated with how to build a strong network.

Mastering networking skills is not so easy, but with the right education and practice, you will become good at using this skill to maximize and grow your business.

Effective Communication Skill

Communication is vital to the success of network marketing business. As you progress in your network marketing business, you will realize that your pattern of communication, with both new and old prospects, has the capacity to grow your business or make your business fail.

So it is vital for anyone that wants to achieve success in network marketing business to acquire the necessary communication skills needed to convince people into buying your product or enrolling under you. Effective communication skill is very vital, because they might come a time in your business when you will need to speak to a lot of people in a big room or seminar, and your ability to effectively communicate with these people and convince them to key in to your presentation can bring a major turnaround to your business and help you succeed very fast.

Another very vital thing you need to get educated about is that communication is not only about you speaking to your prospects, but also knowing how to listen, respond and read the body language of your prospects.

Learn Presentation Skills

Another thing that can help you grow your business and achieve success in network marketing is good presentation skill. Learning presentation skill requires patience and a lot of practice.

Good and effective presentation skills enable you to engage your target audience in a way that they get drawn to you and what you have to offer, helps you learn the act of using live and virtual tools to present your offer to your prospects in a way that they can't resist.

Presentation skills help you to quickly adjust to any environment you find yourself, how to present yourself to your audience, how to use interesting stories to engage your audience, how to appear confident when doing your presentation and how to deliver your offer in a very valuable way to your audience.

Presentation is all about the way you package yourself and your offer to your audience, and if your presentation is not well packaged to convince your audience to buy your offer, you will never achieve the success your desire in network marketing.

So if you don't have this important skill needed to succeed in this line of business, then you have to quickly learn it.

Learn Marketing Skills

Marketing is one of the most vital skills that you need to acquire if you desire to achieve success in network marketing. Marketing in network market involves the process, activities and offerings that you undertake in order to bring your products to your prospective customers.

It is very important that you learn marketing skills, and one of the best ways to acquire this education is to spend adequate time with your sponsor, or anyone that has achieved success in network marketing to teach you the type of marketing skills they use to succeed. If you do this, you will learn the marketing skills that work, and avoid those that don't work.

Another way you can acquire the necessary marketing skills is study what the masters of network marketing did, and implement such marketing tactics on your own prospects.

Acquiring the right education from your sponsors/mentors, and studying the marketing tactics of the masters in network marketing, will save you time, money and effort.

Time Management And Planning Skills

Time is money. Time is fleeting and irreversible, that means effective time management and planning is a vital skill you need to acquire if you want to achieve success in network marketing.

As your journey into network marketing progresses, you will realize that there are some activities you engage in that are time wasters and unproductive, and you need to learn how to avoid them or manage them effectively otherwise they will become the obstacles that'll stand in the way of your success in network marketing. These time-wasting activities are unnecessary and unsolicited calls and visits, unproductive meetings, social media notifications and messages that disturb the flow of work and, etc.

Time is the most effective tool you have when you are running and managing your own business, and network marketing is not an exception, so you must learn how to effectively plan and manage your time in order to succeed. You must learn how to prioritize your activities according to importance by having a time management log.

There Is A Process To Follow

Network marketing business is a very organized business that requires you to follow some process in order to succeed. Your ability to diligently follow this process will determine how well and quick you achieve your desired success in this business model.

Some of the processes to follow in network marketing to achieve the success you desire include:

Look For A Reputable Company To Join

If your aim is to succeed in network marketing, then you need to carefully search for a good and reputable network marketing company to join. That means that you have to do your research and necessary due diligence in seeking out a company that offers the type of quality and value driven products you would be happy to market, offers the type of support and logistics that can help you grow and succeed in network marketing and offer the type of compensation plan that can compensate for your time, effort and investment.

Avoid companies with bad reputation and bad products, even if their compensation plan looks nice and enticing.

Enroll Under A Reliable And Honest Sponsor

This is a very vital aspect in network marketing, and it should be taken seriously. The reason is that, the success you will enjoy in this business and how long it will take before that success comes largely depends on how reliable and honest your sponsor is.

So don't be in a hurry to just come into network marketing because of the good success stories that you have heard about the business, but follow the process of searching for a reliable and honest sponsor to enroll with, and that sponsor will be your mentor that will guide you and teach you the necessary skills and steps to follow in order to achieve the success you desire.

Learn More

Knowledge is the key factor that determines how far you will go in network marketing and the level of success you will enjoy. So, be humble and patient to go through the process of acquiring the basic education that will guarantee your success in this business. Learn from your sponsor. Do research to learn about the industry best practices and the latest ways to effectively market your products and present your offer to your prospects.

Principles To Follow

Network marketing, like any other lucrative business has guiding principles that guarantee success. It is not that if you don't follow the principles you will fail in this business, but following the principles is the surest way to grow your business, maximize the potential in you, and achieve the financial freedom you desire in this business model.

Since the inception of network marketing, many network marketing companies have come and gone, there have been changes to payment plans, the products/services differ, but the guiding principles that have guaranteed the success of many in this line of business remains the same.

So, no matter who you are or what country you are from, if you apply the same principles, you will see the same level of success that those successful people saw and enjoyed.

Below are the principles that guarantee success in network marketing business:

Hanging out with people with a positive and success driven mindset

Do you want to enjoy success in all that you do in life, network marketing inclusive? Then you need to start associating with the type of people who passes the right positive and success driven mindset that will propel you to succeed.

Eagles don't fly in the same altitude as vultures; neither do lions move in the same group with hyenas. So if you hang out with negative and pessimistic people, you need to do way with them if you want to enjoy success in network marketing.

If your friend or your network of associates dislike network marketing, and they don't believe that you can become successful in this business, then you have no reason to be in that group if you want to pursue your business growth and success in network marketing. This is because they will discourage you, derail all your efforts and make sure you fail.

Get Specialized Skills

Look around you, and honestly ask yourself why the most educated people are not the richest people around you, or why the richest people in the world are not the most educated people? Or why even two people with the same level of education have different success/wealth rate? Do you think is by luck or having a better destiny? The answer is big no!

The simple reason for this is the acquisition of specialized skills, skills tailored toward making money and become rich. This specialized skills are not taught in school; they are acquired through mentorship, reading and watching motivational materials, attending seminars and reading books about people that became successful in your field.

So if you want to achieve success in network marketing, then you need to have a mentor, read books about people that became successful in this business and apply the principles they applied and attend seminars.

Believe That Only Success Is Your Destination

We are a product of our thoughts and belief system. Therefore, from the very first day you make up your mind to be a part of the network marketing family, see yourself destined to succeed, and do everything needed to succeed.

With this type of positive and success driven mindset, there is nothing that comes your way that you can't subdue and overcome.

"Believing that you can, develops the power that can" - Norman Vincent Pearle.

Don't Stop Learning And Developing Yourself

The importance of learning and developing yourself to get maximum success in this line of business cannot be overemphasized. Don't stop learning, but continuously keep looking for new ways and methods to improve your business, new marketing strategies and new ways to make your offer irresistible.

There is Cause for Alarm if you are Poor as a Network Marketer

Network marketing is a well packaged and structured business model that can make you rich, all you need is to come into the business with a positive and right attitude, find a good and reliable company that offers great and quality products, develop a good marketing strategy to sell those products and you will become rich.

People who have negative stories of failure to tell about network marketing, are not telling you the whole truth about what actually made them fail. The truth is that their failure was their inability to harness the abundant potential in network marketing and leverage on the support provided by the network marketing company to succeed.

Network marketing as a business model is a real, legitimate and lucrative business that provides people with quality and value driven products that solve problems at good prices. So making money through network is because of the products they provide, but the financial success of the people that made it is as a result of their dedication, hard work, skills and patience applied to build a system that effectively sells products.

Network marketing gives you the opportunity to grow and multiply your success by helping other people to grow and succeed as well. Network marketing is a network of success if well practiced and implemented, and it gets better and easier with technology because you can now use automated marketing software and techniques such as Facebook marketing and other social networks to grow and expand your network.

So if you are into network marketing and you are poor, then there is a cause for alarm, and the fault is entirely yours, because there are a lot of incentives, support, training, mentorship, and the quality products offered by network marketing companies to help you succeed and become rich.

Nothing Ventured, Nothing Gained

Success is a function of sowing and reaping, planting and harvesting. There is nothing like nothing for something in business, and network marketing is not different. The level of success you will enjoy is as a result of the income, time and effort that you are willing to invest.

If you have seen or heard the success stories of successful network marketers, and you are still skeptical and unwilling to come on board because of some of the negative stories you have heard about the business, just know that you can't know for sure unless you venture into the business.

And for those that are already into network marketing, but are afraid to venture deeper, by investing more money, time and effort needed to succeed, just know that the gain you will get from network marketing is function of what you are willing to invest.

Nothing ventured, nothing gained. There is no business without risk. So, rather than sitting on the sidelines speculating about network marketing, venture into this lucrative business and reap the benefits that others have. Success is for the brave hearted; it is for men and women who are willing and ready to take the risk and venture into any business with the determination to succeed against all odds.

People that never take advantage of opportunity to venture into new areas of business, or make the necessary moves to succeed due to fear never go far in life. You need to develop a "Can-Do" mentality to achieve any meaningful and lasting success in life.

For every success there is a price to pay, and without taking the bold decision to venture into any good business like network marketing, your chances of making it in life are slim.

Quitters Never Win and Winners Never Quit

There is no business venture that doesn't have its own peculiar problems, and network marketing, despite how well packaged and organized it is, has some things that might present challenges to a network marketer if not well managed.

Just like any other business, such problems can be minimized, curtailed and overcome in order to achieve success. But if you are the type that quits at the sight of any little problem, then you are not psychologically and emotionally primed for success. Quitters never win; they are not patient enough to apply the power of determination, diligence and perseverance to overcome any obstacle they meet in doing business.

For you to achieve your desired success in network marketing, you must have the mentality of a winner, a strong 'I can do it' mentality that makes you determine never to quit in the face of challenges and obstacles.

Perseverance to the end should be the motto of anyone that wants to succeed in network marketing. This is because network marketing involves meeting people one on one, or in group to present your products to them, and try to convince them to enroll into the marketing company you are already working with, and some might reject your offer or even behave as if what you are selling is not valuable. But if you don't possess the power of perseverance to withstand these rejections, you will become emotional defeated and quit the business.

One of the major keys to success in network marketing business is the power of perseverance. Most of the successful people you see or hear of in network marketing did not get there by chance or luck, they faced a lot of obstacles, overcame those challenges; they didn't quit, they held on strongly and they became the winners that they are today.

The truth is that, no matter the amount of money you invest into network marketing, the level of education you acquire in order to succeed, the type of sponsor/mentor that you have, the time you spend to succeed, if you don't crown those efforts with perseverance and develop the can-do mentality to succeed, you will never achieve your desired success in network marketing.

Let me reiterate the importance of perseverance with this quote from Calvin Coolidge,

"Nothing in this world can take the place of persistence. Talent will not; nothing is more common than unsuccessful men with talent. Genius will not; unrewarded genius is almost a proverb. Education will not; the world is full with educated derelicts. Persistent and determination alone are omnipotent".

So now that we have established that perseverance is a key factor for success in network marketing, let us now look into how you can use this strategy (perseverance) in your network marketing business.

Develop A Long Term Mindset

A lot of people quit easily in network marketing because they have a short sight and get rich quick mindset when they came into the business. Short sight and get rich quick is the business mentality of losers and small thinkers. The successful people you know are long term thinkers, who use the power of perseverance to build their network marketing business from the scratch. They were not afraid to face obstacles and never considered quitting. And if you want to succeed like them, you have to develop a long term mindset and persevere to the end.

Eliminate The Negative Mindset And Emotion That Attract Failure

Having a negative mindset and emotion are some of the things that lead to failure in network marketing. Negative mindset and emotions comes in the form of self-doubt and self-rejection, and the way to overcome this and achieve success in network marketing is to apply the power of perseverance and determination.

Network with other marketers that are determined to succeed

This is very important to the success of your networking business. Surround yourself with winners and positive minded network marketers, people that are hungry for success, people that will fill you with positive energy and knowledge to become successful in your business.

The Road To Success Is For Men With Faith

Have faith and believe in yourself. Believing in your ability to maximize your God-given potential is a major key to succeed in a business like network marketing.

One of the biggest differences between the people who succeed in life and the ones, who fail, is not necessarily lack of intelligence, lack of opportunity or lack of finance, but the faith and self-belief that they have to achieve their goals and fulfill their dreams.

Norman Vincent Pearle said ''Believing that you can, develops the power that can." This saying holds true for anyone that desires success in network marketing. You need to have unwavering faith in your ability to succeed, and approach every business prospect with the mindset of a winner.

Let us be honest here, if you don't have faith in your ability to build a successful network marketing business, who else will have faith in you? Who will key in to the vision of a man without faith? You have to believe that your business has the capacity to grow and succeed before others will buy into your vision.

Having faith in whatever you do propels you to aim high, set goals and withstand any obstacle that comes on your way to success. Without faith there will be no motivation, and without motivation, you can't muster the efforts you need to succeed, and without efforts your failure is certain.

Faith builds the necessary confidence you need to reach out to others and market your products and present your offer to new prospects, and if you lack confidence, no one will believe in you and what you have to offer.

Having faith and believing in yourself and in your ability to succeed is important because it helps you to:

- Recognize that you have the God-given ability to set and accomplish your business goals.

- You become very optimistic about the future of your business because you possess the faith to withstand and overcome any obstacle that comes your way.

- Develop "I-can-do-it" mentally that is vital to the success of your business.

- Develop the motivation to accomplish your business dreams.

- Attract like-minded and success driven business colleagues.

- Don't let fear define who you become, and determine the level of success you will enjoy in life. "When your back is to the wall and you are facing fear head on the only way is forward and through it. – (**Stephen Richards**)

What it takes to succeed is in-built in you from birth. All you have to do to maximize that in-built potential to succeed is to sit down, meditate to awaken that sleeping potential and then fight for the success you desire, because the success you desire will not fight for you.

The term impossibility means nothing. The moment a man sets his mind and determines to achieve something, there is nothing that can stop him from achieving it. The success you will achieve is a function of your mindset. When your mind is set on a goal, you develop, you grow and success embraces you.

So don't let some of the negative stories that you have heard about network marketing from people who didn't apply the basic principles of success in this business scare you away or make you lose faith. You have to come into this business with faith and self-belief and you will surely achieve the success you desire.

Poverty Is A Risk; Wealth Is A Risk

In life, we are all entitled to the choices we make, but we have to live with the consequences of the choices we make.

Life generally requires some degree of risk, it doesn't matter the divide you find yourself. To be poor is a decision that requires risk, and to be rich and wealthy requires some risk too, so you are free to choose the type of risk you will love to be involved with.

But before you choose the risk that leads to poverty, you have to be fully aware of the consequences of your decision.

Poverty brings shame, lack, loss of self-value, insecurity, emotional and psychological trauma, lack of choice and other socioeconomic problems.

Wealth and riches gives you self-worth and respect, financial and material security, a voice, a wide range of choices, attracts opportunities that will make you even richer, peace of mind and happiness.

So, today be mindful of what you choose for yourself and even for your family. Yes, because that wrong decision you make today, and that risk to become rich and wealthy that you refused, or too ignorant to make today might make your family suffer the pain and humiliation of poverty for generations to come.

But the right decision to join a lucrative and life changing business like network marketing, can secure the financial future of yourself and your family, and make you live a wealthy and prosperous life.

If your aim is to succeed and fight poverty out of your life, then you have to start doing what successful people do. You have to start taking the needed risks to succeed and become rich. Success is a destination, and it requires the right journey to get to that address, but if you are afraid to take risks, or afraid to venture into the right business you will never arrive at that address. But if you are determined and persistent, and take the risk involved, you will surely arrive at that destination. Yes, it might take some time, but you will surely get there.

Don't be someone that gives too many excuses why you should not take a risk, or procrastinate and wait for the right time to take risk. Yesterday, you gave all the "sweet" reasons you will take the needed risk to become rich tomorrow, today is that tomorrow you talked about yesterday. So, what are you still waiting for, and what is your excuse for not taking action today?

In (Proverbs 24:33-34), the Bible says,

"Yet a little sleep, a little slumber, a little folding of the hands to sleep. So shall poverty come as one that travelled, and thy want as an armed man?"

The excuses that you give today will be responsible for the poverty that you will suffer tomorrow. So choose wisely.

The more the analysis, the more the paralysis (Analysis Paralysis)

Decision making is one of the most important factors that determine success in life. Quick, well detailed and analyzed decision can propel us to the level of success we desire in any venture, especially in the field of business. However, delayed, over analyzed and rationalized decision making can rob us the impetus and zeal that we need to proceed in our business journey.

Analysis paralysis is a pattern of thinking, over analyzing and over planning something or a venture which leads to indecision or inaction. It limits the outcome of a venture and makes you unable to make a decision or take action.

It leads to indecision, fear of making a move and fear of failure. It causes decline in productivity and waste of productive time and energy, it kills your creativity and robs you of the will power to venture and succeed. Analysis paralysis creates fear where there should be action, it raises doubt where there should be faith to proceed and win.

If your aim is to achieve success in any venture you find yourself or that you have keen interest in, then you have to kill that indecision factor in your life and avoid analysis paralysis. Instead of wasting valuable time and delaying your progress due to indecision, use the information and resources at your disposal now and just proceed. If there is any issue that arises along the way, you would have learnt valuable lessons to effectively deal with them.

If analysis paralysis has held you captive and robbed you of the zeal to venture and succeed in any field you find yourself, try the following tips to free yourself:

- Don't strive for perfection. Go excellence instead.
- Accept that failure is a possibility, but that you have the ability to overcome it and come out stronger and successful.

- Understand that the simple and less complex solutions are most times the best solutions.

- Trust your intuition and core values, and let your faith and self-belief be your guiding light.

- Know that fear is at the core of every indecision. So, deal with it and move on in faith.

- The time to start is now. Stop procrastinating and focus your time and energy on getting started.

- Set achievable goals and create timelines to achieve them.

- Don't accept failure as destination. Focus on succeeding, and you surely will.

If analysis paralysis is limiting your progress and defining the type of life you live, you need to quickly get rid of such negative pattern so that you can make timely and informed decisions in order not to lose valuable opportunities.

If you have been wanting to come on board and enjoy the abundant benefits in network marketing, but fear of the unknown and indecision has kept you back from being among the many men and women that have grown their business and become very successful and financially free through network marketing, then this is the time to get rid of that fear and become part of the successful family of network marketers.

Financial Freedom Is Not By Chance, It Is By Choice

A lot of people go through life wishing and hoping that one day, by a stroke of luck, they will become rich and financially free. They think financial freedom will one day happen to them by chance.

But wishes don't grow on trees and if "wishes were horses even beggars would ride." Financial freedom is not something that you wish for or something that can happen to you by chance; you have to actively choose to become financially free.

It is a positive action that requires hard work, determination and perseverance to achieve.

Every man or woman you see today enjoying financial freedom did not achieve it by chance, or by sitting idle wishing and hoping that one day fortune will smile on them and they would become rich. That is the attitude of wishful thinkers and lazy people who never do well in life. Successful people achieve financial freedom by choosing to make financial decisions that contribute to their success, by working hard and smart, taking the necessary risks involved and doing business that brought them financial freedom.

Achieving financial freedom is not determined by tribe, color of your skin or status. It is a function of the choices and decisions you make. You can't control where you were born, the family you are born into and when you are born. But you can control your choices, the financial choices you make, and you can control the level of success you enjoy by choosing to have faith in your inbuilt

abilities and diligently work hard and smart to achieve financial freedom.

Let us take a look at some very motivating and inspiration quotes on making choices.

"Life is a matter of choices, and every choice you make makes you." - John C. Maxwell.

"Everything in your life is a reflection of a choice you have made. If you want different result, make a different choice." – (Anonymous)

"May your choices reflect your hopes, not your fears." - Nelson Mandela.

"You are free to make whatever choices you want, but you are not free from the consequences of the choice." – (Anonymous)

"Every morning you have two choices: Continue to sleep with your dreams or

wake up and chase your dreams. The choice is yours." – (Anonymous)

"I believe we are solely responsible for our choices, and we have to accept the consequences of every deed, word, and thought throughout our lifetime." - Elisabeth Kubler-Ross.

"You always have two choices: your commitment versus your fear." - Sammy Davis Jr.

"Choices are the hinges of destiny." - Edwin Markham.

"Every choice you make has an end result." - Zig Ziglar.

"Destiny is no matter of chance. It is a matter of choice. It is not a thing to be waited for, it is a thing to be achieved." - Williams Jennings Bryan.

So, if you desire financial freedom, don't sit idle and hope that one day the chance for a breakthrough will come. It will never come. You have to make the choice to become financially free, because the financial choice you make today will determine the level of financial freedom you will enjoy tomorrow. Be courageous and brave in making the right choices.

Your Destiny Is In Your Hands

"Whatever the heart can conceive and believe it can achieve." - Napoleon Hill

A lot of people live with the belief that providence or luck will shape their lives and determines who they become, but the truth is that your destiny and what you will become in life totally lies in your hand.

There is no miracle that will determine your financial destiny when you are lazy and unproductive; there is no luck in building a vision, or growing that mega business that can change your destiny, the building of good financial destiny lies in your hand. You need to rise up now and take the necessary action required to fulfill your destiny.

A great motivational book writer Tony Robbins said, "Your success is 80% psychological and 20% fundamental. In essence, he is saying that if you cultivate the right mindset and psychology needed to succeed, your success will be guaranteed.

Your mind and how you apply it is the greatest asset and ally you need to succeed. On the other hand, your mind can be your biggest enemy and the militating factor against your success if you apply it negatively. Every human being has great potential, but the belief system we grow up with either limits our success or gives us limitless potential.

Great men who achieved great success in their various fields were not born with a more developed or advanced brain, but they developed themselves, worked hard and smart, believed in their ability to succeed and made the right choices and decisions needed to succeed.

If you possess a burning desire to succeed, a strong dream and vision, and a positive mindset then your success is inevitable. If your aim is to succeed against all odds, and chart the course of your destiny with your own hands then follow the actions steps enumerated below:

- Have a strong faith and believe in yourself and your abilities to succeed.
- Be determined, consistent and persistent in pursuing your dreams and working towards your set goals. Remember winners never quit, and quitters never win.
- Daily load yourself with positive, motivational educational materials and study what other successful people do.
- Make friends and keep the company of people who will motivate, build and elevate you.
- Manage your time effectively.
- Take positive actions to achieve your heart desire, and don't allow too much planning

and rationalizing delay you or deny you from taken action.

Our destinies are not fixed somewhere, neither is it written in the stars, under the earth or in the wind. We have the capacity to plant, water and nurture the events that will shape our future and determine our financial destiny.

Chapter 4: Why People Fail In Network Marketing Business

Lack Of Professionalism

Professionalism can aid the growth of a business, or when it is lacking, mar its growth and success. This is due to the fact that customers love to patronize people and businesses that have credibility and act professionally in the way they do business and offer their services.

People want to have assurance that the products and services they are paying for are actually what it is presented to be or served the purpose that it promises to.

Professionalism in business has to do with adhering to the core values and principles that govern a business. It guides how you present a product or a service, who you present it to, when you present it, and how credible your presentation is.

Professionalism is the reason you will never see a medical doctor offer his services to a total stranger, or see him distributing flyers showcasing his services on the street, neither will you see him unprofessionally forcing people to come to his clinic for treatments and checkups, no. They have a set business and professional standard, and they follow it diligently in doing their business.

Let us now take a look at social media platforms, with Facebook as a case study. Has there been any time when you got a notification or private message from your doctor wanting to know when you will come in for a medical checkup or for a treatment because you need it? Or have you seen a doctor spamming your inbox and tagging the pictures of his business? No, they don't act that unprofessionally, and the reasons are simple.

This is because that way of doing business is unacceptable, unprofessional, annoying and psychologically insulting to the customers. If doctors adopt those unprofessional methods of doing business, prospective clients will not value their services and they will lose credibility and respect.

This unprofessional way of doing business and recruiting new prospects is what a lot of distributors in network marketing do. Due to lack of professionalism, these distributors have resorted in using ineffective, annoying, tacky, outdated and below-standard advertising methods to market their products and recruit new prospects.

This unwholesome and unprofessional method of doing business has brought a lot of negative reviews and damaged the reputation of network marketing.

Lack of professionalism on the part of some distributors has become one of the major reasons why some people have stayed away from network marketing and refused to explore the abundant opportunities in this lucrative business model.

Professionalism is regarded as an essential part of every business, and network marketing is not an exception, and if your aim is to become successful and grow your business then you should make professionalism an integral part of your business.

Professionalism integrates and harmonizes all the facets of a good business, which include business operations, customer care and relations and advertisement.

Lack Of Credibility

"Credibility is a business leader's currency; with it, he or she is solvent; without it; he or she is bankrupt." – John Maxwell

Any business or business person who wants to succeed should cultivate certain qualities that'll enable him to grow his business and achieve his desired success. Some of those qualities are customer trust, market credibility, customer confidence and a good business reputation.

Humans beings are networkers by nature and they rely on certain attributes like honesty, transparency and integrity in choosing who they network with. The truth is that some network marketers don't operate their business in a credible way, and this makes some people place network marketers on the same level as scammers and con artists, but this this is not true.

The reason people see network marketers as scammers and con artists is mainly due to the popular business dogma that "Everyone is your prospect." Though it is not wrong to leverage on opportunities to market your product and get a new prospect to enroll with you, but wisdom and moderation should be the key.

This negative business dogma has made some network marketers to employ embarrassing and idiotic antics like harassment and deception to make their products and present their offer. A lot of people have heard horror stories about network marketing, and that is because some network marketers who lack credibility has given a new prospect a false impression and expectation about how easy network marketing is, and how easy you can become rich through this business model, only for them to discover that all they have been told are lies and they have been set up to fail. So, these people will feel deceived and scammed, and quit the business with horrible stories which they share with everyone they meet.

For anyone who wants to succeed in network marketing, it is vital for the person to build a business anchored on credibility, trust, and this entails recruiting new prospect responsibly, promise less and deliver more, be honest with your prospect and let them understand that network marketing is not a get rich quick scheme, but that with hard work, determination and the right training they will surely become very successful.

Network marketing business like most traditional businesses is anchored on relationships, and those relationships are built on trust and for you to effectively maintain that trust, you must exhibit credibility. As a network marketing distributor, you can't anchor your business on lies and deception, you have to let your word be your bond and be accountable to customers and prospects.

Ways To Build Credibility In Network Marketing Business

- **Honesty**

  One thing that can destroy your credibility, your business and make you experience failure in network marketing is dishonesty. Lying and presenting your products and offers with deception and misrepresentation might make you win some customers and recruit prospects at first, but in the long run it will bring doom to your business.

  Customers and prospects love to do business with someone who is honest and transparent, and if you possess these qualities, you will have positive reviews which will attract more people to you and help to build your business. So, be honest and build credibility and success will surely come.

- **Be Very Sensitive**

  Develop and demonstrate sensitivity and empathy for your customers and prospects. Don't just look at them as a tool or avenue to make money and grow your business. See them as partners in progress, and care about their needs, wants and desires.

- **Be Value Driven And Knowledgeable**

  Be knowledgeable about the products you offer and the company you represent. This will make people have confidence in you, and key in to what you have to offer.

  The truth is that no one will want to deal with a distributor who doesn't offer a value driven product, and lacks the working knowledge of the products he is selling and the company he is working with.

Lack Of Consistency

Consistency is the difference between success and failure in anything that we do in life. In business, it is inevitable.

It is very difficult, if not impossible, to measure the workability and efficiency of a marketing method if it is not done consistently. It has been established that business growth and success is a function of consistency, but how can any business drive growth and monitor success if it is constantly changing and shifting from one business tactics to the other.

One of the barriers to success in network marketing is lack of consistency. This is because different teams and individuals have their own marketing tactics which they teach their people and implement.

What team A is teaching and implementing is totally different from what team B is teaching and implementing, and this form of inconsistency will never support the growth of network marketing and drive success.

Consistency in network marketing is not only about the tactics and methods implemented to drive sales and grow your business; it is also about being focused and staying on course when things don't go according to plan.

Lack of consistency is the main reason some network marketers move from one network marketing company to another. Whereas the network marketing companies might not be the cause of their failure, rather it is their impatience and inability to focus and be consistent in building their business over a period of time.

Some people come into network marketing wanting to hit the ground running and achieve success immediately, but when the success they seek elude them after a month or two, they run away thinking it is the company or its method of marketing of the company that is the problem, but the actual problem lies in their lack of consistency.

Lack Of Marketing Skill

Marketing skill is one of the most important skills anyone who desires success in network marketing needs to acquire, practice and perfect.

A lot of people were deceived into network marketing by unscrupulous distributors who told them that they don't need marketing skills to succeed, that in fact they don't need to sell their products; all they need to do to achieve success was to share their products to people.

But this is a lie, and the truth is that if you are into network marketing you are in sales. For you to build a successful network marketing business, you must learn, practice and master the act of sales.

It doesn't matter what anyone has told you in the past, or what format they use to get you to enroll into network marketing, the truth you need to know is that network marketing is about selling.

It is therefore very crucial that you master this skill as it will determine the level of success you will enjoy.

Sales are at the heart of every business, and without sales the business will fizzle out and die. Don't be deceived, every single business on earth thrives on sales, and network marketing is not an exception, so when someone tells you that sharing your products alone without selling can guarantee you success in network marketing, that person is deceiving you.

You have to influence people to buy the products you have and become a member of your team, and that is selling. You must have the ability to effectively walk to people through your offer and convince them to key into it, and that is selling.

A lot of people in network marketing don't like to use the word selling, or see themselves as salespeople, but they should understand that selling is the same thing as influencing people, selling is actually about getting your prospect to see something from your own point of view, see the value of what you have to offer and take the needed action.

Marketing and selling is noble, it is a means of presenting workable solutions to people's needs and problems, it requires the right knowledge, attitude, skills, and right personality to achieve success.

To be in selling, you need to study the psychology of buyers, and understand the mental process that people go through before they buy and when buying. You need to know that humans are stingy in nature and they love to hold on to money than spending it. So, it takes adequate convincing, packaging, value presentation for them to buy, and that is where marketing skills comes into play.

Sharing alone will never guarantee you success in this line of business. You need to learn sales skills, practice and master it as this will have a great effect on your success.

Lack Of Commitment

Some people come into network marketing thinking it is a gold mine where they will apply little effort, commit little time and resources and hit it big in a few months. But when all of these don't happen, and when other expectations they had when coming into network marketing fail, they blame the company, the system and every other thing they assumed caused their failure, but themselves.

The truth is that if you want to see growth and enjoy success in your network marketing business, you have to fully commit to its success. That means giving it all you have got in terms of time, effort and finance.

Network marketing is a business, and it has to be treated as such, so if your desire is to build a successful business in network marketing, you have to be fully committed to the growth and success of your business, and that means committing a minimum of 10 to 15 hours every week to see the level of success you desire.

These 10 to 15 hours should be committed judiciously to activities that will improve your business and produce income. You should also commit adequate time to training, research, networking with other network marketers and other productive activities that will grow and position your business for success.

It is very important to come into network marketing with a vision and set goals of what you want to achieve, and to have a mental picture of where you want your business to be at a particular time, but you have to commit your time, effort and income to see your vision come true.

Money is indeed needed to start a network marketing business, but if you come in with the mindset that you are going to invest money, relax and see your business grow and become successful, then you need to think again, because to succeed in this business, you need more than money. You need to be fully committed.

Lack Of Money

Network marketing is a business that requires capital to start and run the business effectively. You don't just need money to get enrolled and get your starter kits, you also need money for training, research and personal development that will enhance the success of your network marketing business.

Though the money required to start and successfully run a network marketing business is not as much as the money needed to run a traditional business, but some people still say they don't have money to join the business opportunity.

These types of people are categorized into two groups. The first group is those who have genuine interest in the business opportunity, and would love to be part of the business opportunity, but can't afford it due to the present economic situation. The second group of people are the ones have money to join the business opportunity, but they are not really interested in it, so they give the excuse of not having money, because they don't want to offend you or hurt your feelings.

Money is the lifeblood of any business, and it is the oil that ensures the smooth running of all the component of the business, and this applies to network marketing. So if you want to achieve success in this business, you have to be ready to spend money to see it grow and flourish.

Lack Of Knowledge

Knowledge and understanding of a business model, as well as the skillset needed to succeed is very important for the growth, development and success of the business and this applies to network marketing as well.

One of the problems people face in network marketing which makes them fail is their lack of understanding and knowledge of the business model. Due to lack of understanding and the basic knowledge of this business model, some people think that network marketing is just:

- Join a network marketing company/network marketing business.
- Showcase your products and plans to people in your close network, like family, friends and colleagues.
- Convince them to join the business opportunity.
- Then start making big money.

This is the concept that some network marketing distributors have deceptively sold to some people that makes them join the business with enthusiasm, but which they later found out to be untrue. Some network marketers have made a lot of people skeptical and afraid due to the wild and absurd claims they make while trying to recruit a new prospect, and these negative behaviors have made others that had interest in this business opportunity to conclude that network marketing is a scam and a business of deceptive people.

But network marketing is not a scam, it is a business model that has the capacity to make you financially independent if you stay committed and take time to acquire the working knowledge and understanding of how the business model works.

For you to achieve success in network marketing, you should understand the truth about the business, have the basic knowledge about the company you intend to join, the business model of the company, the year the company was founded, the success rate of the company, their products and the marketing concept of the company.

The earning and success you will enjoy in network marketing is a function of the knowledge you acquire, so take the time to learn how to invite new prospect, how to effectively do your presentation and close sales.

Learn from your sponsor/mentor and learn from your seniors in network marketing business.

Chapter 5: Some Lies People Tell Themselves About Network Marketing

A lot of people have filled up their mind with lies and misconception of what network marketing is about, and how the business model works, but this information they have about network marketing is false.

So with this misconception and misinformation they have about this business model, they tell themselves some lies such as:

- I don't like knocking on people's door or cold calling.
- I don't have the ability to convince people or push them to buy or accept my offer.
- I am not good at marketing or selling of products.
- I feel awkward and shy about talking and presenting my offer and products to people.

- I lack people-skills to build a networking relationship.

- I am not educated enough and lack the knowledge needed to succeed in this line of business.

But all these excuses are lies that people tell themselves for not wanting to be part of this great marketing opportunity that has the capacity to change their lives and make them financially free.

The truth is that network marketing is not just about sales and making money, it is about offering value driven products that solve problems and provide the daily needs of man. So you need to stop seeing network marketing as a means to make sales and generate income for yourself, but as an avenue to help others and proffer solutions to their problem.

Network marketing is not pushing people to buy your product, or become an aggressive street hustler. It is about targeting the right audience that needs the solution your products provide, and offer them the solutions through your products. Once you are able to identify the right audience, selling will happen easily.

Selling your product become pushing and hustling when you are presenting your products to the wrong audience, people who have no need for your product.

Network marketing is not as difficult as some misinformed people present it, and for you to be successful, you must develop the core values needed to succeed.

The core values needed to become successful in network marketing are:

You Have To Believe In The Company You Want To Enroll With

Before you enroll with a network marketing company you must believe in the working model of the company. You must study that company and find out if they have the right foundation and finance to help them achieve their business goals, if the company has the right management that can drive business growth and ensure the business and financial future you desire. It is very important to choose the right company that you can strongly believe in, because when you do, all the lies that you tell yourself about networking business will stop and you can confidently join the business and achieve success.

So how do you determine the right company that guarantees the success you desire? The following steps will guide you:

- The right company should be the one that have been effectively operating for a minimum of five years, and have a good record of growth and success.
- A company that offers value-driven products that you love and passionate about. Products that you feel confident and excited to sell and share with people.
- Company that has a compensation plan that is driving growth and success for the company and the distributors.

- Does the company have good and efficient marketing tools offline and online that helps their distributors grow, such as a corporate website and marketing website?
- Does the company have excellent training program designed to help their distributors grow?

You have to believe in the products that the company has to offer.

Like I mentioned in the early chapters, network marketing is not all about sharing your products with your friends, family and people in your close network. It involves selling of products and presentation of offers to the right audience, and failure to do this is why some people tell themselves lies about network marketing.

The criteria for choosing the right products to sell and share to people should include:

The products must be the ones that you have passion for.

- The products must be value-driven to provide solution to the problem of the customers.

- The product must have a mass appeal.

- The products must be affordable.

- The products should be such that people buy all the time. That means repeated purchase is a must.

- The products should easy and simple to use.

If all these factors are in place and you chose the right company that offers the right products, all those lies that you tell yourself about not liking to knock on people's door, don't like to push people, not good at selling and feeling awkward talking to people about your product or service and business opportunity will become a thing of the past, because at that point you will enjoy what you are doing and become a problem solver, not just a seller.

You Have To Believe In Network Marketing As A Business Model

People that tell themselves lies about network marketing don't have passion for the business and they don't believe in the business model. For you to stop telling yourself those lies about network marketing, you need to have absolute belief in the business model. You need to understand that network marketing is a legitimate, big business opportunity that is capable of giving the success you desire and make you financially independent and free. Once you develop this mindset about network marketing, all your fears and the lies you tell about the business will vanish.

Have you asked yourself why some of the richest men on earth are into network marketing? Billionaires like Warren Buffet, Richard Branson and Donald Trump with a host of others? The answer is that network marketing is one of the most lucrative and success driven business in the world right now, and it is an established fact that goods and services worth $169 USD are distributed through network marketing in more than 100 countries all over the world.

Do you really think billionaires like Warren Buffet, Donald Trump and Richard Branson will get themselves in network marketing if the business model was a scam and not yielding the desired result? The answer is a big NO.

So stop telling yourself lies today and join these billionaires to become part of the successful network marketing family.

You Have To Believe In Yourself And In Your Ability To Succeed

Some of those lies that people tell themselves for not wanting to be a part of the success that network marketing is mainly because they don't believe in themselves and in their ability to succeed.

For you to develop self-belief and conquer the fear that has limited you and made you to fill your head with lies about what you can do and can't do, you need to start developing yourself, because self-development is a major key to success.

So, start developing yourself by attending events and seminars where you will be trained on the skills needed to succeed in network marketing, events and conferences organized by network marketing companies. Affiliate yourself with a mentor and leaders in network marketing, and read self-development books.

When all these are done and you have acquired self-belief you will realize that those lies you have been telling yourself about network marketing are unfounded and you will be able to key into the business opportunity with the needed confidence and mindset to succeed.

The truth is that the people around you and the society you belong, don't care if you possess the ability to succeed, they will even prefer to see you remain where you are presently and they will tell you to play safe and not venture into what they personally consider risky. They will tell you stories about the people that failed in network marketing, but they will not tell you that those people did not follow the core values that I have listed about that guarantee success in network marketing.

Chapter 6: Why Network Marketing Might Not Be For You

Network marketing is one business that offers maximum opportunities for the average person without a lot of money to invest in becoming free financially free. Network Marketing is the circulation of products and services via a network of independent representatives. Each representative is responsible for consuming a small number of products, and recruits others to do likewise. The volume of sales is generated through a lot of people each month buying and selling a small number of products. Commissions are paid based on recruiting new distributors and consumption of the products and services within the network. A company that offers products or services provide network to remove the need for costly advertisement. By deploying a system of marketers and also get paid for distributing products they like with others through word of mouth. Network Marketing gets you paid over and over for working one. Network marketing may be a place for many because people are not in search of products, services, or even business opportunities; they're looking for solutions to life's problems. Hence they tend to dive into any available means that can put food on their table.

The internet has made people interested in network marketing. The internet's now helps network marketers build national and international businesses from the comfort of their homes. The internet has helped people to be able to work from their home, and within a short time, build a large business. The income generated from this business will secure their financial future and provide more free time to enjoy life truly.

Nevertheless, some attributes are required for one to become an outstanding network marketer. Some individuals cannot endure some of the things faced by network marketers such as failure, rejection. Hence, this chapter aims at presenting reasons some persons may not be fit for network marketing:

Antisocial

If you are someone that does not like relating with people, that is you are antisocial, then network marketing should not be an area you should consider. Network marketing demands that you possess potential abilities to interact with several people, to convert them to your customers.

Your attitude has the capacity to break or make you in this line of business. If you have an antisocial attitude, then don't ever consider being a network marketer because you will not make any headway. But if you possess a winsome, positive and upbeat social attitude then you can easily get people to listen to your offer, purchase your product and enroll into your business opportunity.

If You Are Not Good With Words

Effective communication is essential in network marketing. It is the area that is unique to the marketer and scares off many from network marketing and therefore requires special consideration.

Marketing involves presenting products or services to potential customers and convincing them to purchase that service or product. Practical communication skills in the form of personal interaction, team communications, are essential attributes of a successful marketer.

Personal Communications

Marketing demands exceptional personal communication skills. Marketers must be extrovert whose aim is to make everyone they work with feel valued, comfortable, and accepted. The sales personnel must generate trust and confidence in themselves as well as the product they represent. They are known for finding the similar ground and making emotional connections with whoever they are dealing with. They make use of their skills in resolving the customer's and company's problems to the good of all.

Team Communications

Network marketers interact every day with a broad diversity of personalities, including company executives, business managers, clients, newspaper journalists, computer scientists and artists. They communicate differently and speak the language unique to their roles. Successful marketers are great at listening and understanding the needs and communications of each type of personality and job position.

Choosing the right words and the ability to convince people to buy or try out your product or service can be a difficulty. Right words are convincing and can go a long way to determine the outcome of your sales. Some marketers do not have confidence in the product and service they offer, and this could turn off the potential customer.

In Nigeria, many potential customers are moved by the persuasive words of marketers and not necessarily the quality of the product or service though that is vital. Hence, if you see effective communication to be challenging, then network marketing is not for you.

You Don't Want To Work

Becoming a business person is not an easy task that is why there are only a few successful entrepreneurs and many job seekers. Entrepreneurship demands hard work, commitment, and a single-minded focus on a goal. The goal of the business is all that the entrepreneur sees and shows unwavering commitment to it. Network marketing is a serious business, and just like any other business that can set you on the path to financial freedom, it requires hard work and dedication.

When you start your network marketing journey, you will undoubtedly encounter challenges, failure, and long hours. You will go through the stress of convincing people to join the business, buy the product or services, but these efforts are worth it, because at the end, you will reap the fruit of your effort. Just as they say in network marketing, you work 70-hour weeks so that you no longer have to work 40 hour weeks!

Don't be deceived by some stories you hear that network marketing is an easy business that can make you rich. Yes, it can make you rich, but only when you are willing and ready to roll up your sleeves and put in the required work that you need to succeed. If you consider this to be too much work, then you are not meant for network marketing.

You Desire To Become A Millionaire Overnight

Network marketing does not guarantee you quick money. This cannot be overemphasized.

Building a network marketing business takes a lot of time, consistency, hard work, and patience.

Network marketing is not a Ponzi scheme and does not give you instant wealth. The more you build, the more you earn. Building is done by introducing more people to the product or service and convincing them enough to purchase the product or service from you. With these four attributes, you have the potential to unlock a significant income source and a rewarding career. If someone tells you a different thing, that person has no idea of network marketing.

You Give Many Excuses

At the base of every excuse is said to be a lack of interest. Excuses show that you are not interested in any business. As earlier stated, network marketing requires all the attention you can give it to overcome the hurdles that come from trying to promote the business. If you consider yourself too busy or lacking sufficient time, have few networks of acquaintances that you can reach out to, or lack money, etc. Then you are probably not good enough for this enterprise. Successful people today in network marketing began their journey, not because they have enough time or money, but because they wanted a solution to create a better life for themselves and other people. So the ball lies in your court, you can have excuses, or you can take a leap of faith.

You Are Not Willing To Give Up Some Things

When you decide to participate in a network marketing business actively, it is not something that you take part in and hope for the best. Building a network marketing business requires you to give up certain old beliefs to embrace a new opportunity. You have to learn to quit self-limiting beliefs and adopt a new attitude and a new mindset. You have to learn to give up your ego and learn from the masters in this business. You have to quit your comfortable office cubicle as well and turn your dining room into your office. You have to give up your comfort zone and step into unchartered waters.

It is going to be very hard at first, and probably you may want to throw in the towel once or twice. It's not easy, but in the beginning, you are going to feel like you are working twice as hard for little or no result. As any of the top income earners of this industry will tell you – but know this, it's worth it!

You Don't Believe In The Company Product Or Services

Product knowledge is an essential sales skill. Understanding the features of your products, grant you the ability to accurately and persuasively present their benefits. Customers enthusiastically respond to sales staff that are passionate about their products and are eager to communicate the profits with them.

Customers are more likely to trust salespeople who show a level of confidence in themselves and what they are marketing. This confidence can be built by increasing your knowledge of your products or services.

It is advisable to be honest with the customer if your product or service has some shortcomings in certain situations. A marketer is known to use knowledge to engage the customers, and lead them through the sales process, and make them have an enjoyable experience that they will want to revisit. Successful salespeople know all of the features of their products and skillfully convert these features into benefits for their customers. These are the essential attributes required for effective network marketing; hence if you don't believe in what your business offers, then network marketing is not for you.

You Need To Invest In Products Of The MLM Company

Investing in the company is essential before you can take part as one of the company's direct selling team. It implies that some investments need to be made before making any gain from the company. But in a situation where you are unable to buy the company's product or pay for services, you can't be part of their MLM team. Therefore, make sure you have sufficient capital is available for this business, and if you lack it, then it is not for you.

Inability To Deal With Failures

Every successful business and business person has experienced one form of failure or the other, but the ability to deal with it is what makes them stand out among their contemporaries.

In the same way, if you cannot cope with failure, then you are not cut out for network marketing. Experts have shown that 97% of network marketers fail at executing their job. And only 3% succeed at it.

A lot of people don't have the capacity to deal with failure, they see it as the end, but actually failure is a stepping stone and learning curve that you can leverage to achieve the success you desire.

''Success is not final, failure is not fatal, it is the courage to continue that counts.'' - Winston Churchill.

The truth is that everyone has failed at one point in their life, or will experience failure at some point in the future, but it is the ability to deal with the failure, pick the valuable lessons and move forward that makes the difference.

As a new entrant into the network marketing business, you might experience some degree of failure at first, but your ability to deal with these failures, learn from them and improve your business is the key to your success. But if you get discouraged, lose interest, complain and lose hope completely because of failure that comes your way, then network marketing is not for you.

Ability To Deal With Rejection

Psychologically and emotionally, rejection is as severe for salespeople, as it is difficult for a hungry cave hunter to trade a rock for a venison steak.

Everybody, at one point or the other, experiences rejection; it is part of life. For salespeople, it is a fact of their work. Therefore, if you want to be successful in network marketing, you must learn to deal with rejection.

Rejection could be brutal sometimes. You can be accused of even promoting a brand that does not conform to environmental, medical or economic standards; some would even also slam the door in your face.

Some potential customers may be having a bad day and thus act rudely, or because of a bad attitude. Your reaction to these situations goes a long way in defining you, as well as determine the success of the product or service you are marketing. You must be outstanding in this area to enhance your marketing. If you are unable to handle rejection, then network marketing is not designed for you.

Tolerance For Lack Of Benefits

In network marketing, privileges such as health care and insurance are absent. The benefit you get if employed fulltime is not given in network marketing. If you are willing to take the risk associated with not being provided with such advantages, then you could proceed with network marketing, otherwise don't.

Though network marketing may not come with the perks and benefits of civil service work or other corporate jobs, but the long term benefits if done properly far exceed any type of benefit that you will get in a conventional job.

In network marketing, you have the chance to grow your business into a multi-million naira business that can employ other people and make you financially free, but in conventional jobs, you remain an employee for life, and retirement benefits that can't guarantee your financial freedom.

The choice is yours. You either wait for benefits and live a life of financial fear and constant lack, or choose business growth through network marketing and enjoy financial freedom.

The Reward

The reward you get from MLM may not be promising at first; it may be far below what you expect from a business when you came on board. And if you expect fast reward for your time and investment, then network marketing as a business model is not for you.

But if you are patient, and put in the needed time and effort to see their business grow and succeed, then network marketing is the ideal business for you. This is because the reward you will get in network marketing (if you are willing to be patient and work hard) far exceed any reward that you will get from most other business.

Chapter 7: Mistakes You Have To Avoid If You Want To Succeed In Network Marketing

It is often advisable while trying to build wealth to have more than one source of income. It is also advisable to create a source of income that gives you passive income. This is money generated without much effort. While network marketing does take some work, when it is done correctly, it also has the potential to earn you passive income.

Multi-level marketing is considered an exciting trend in business today. It is a business that offers more opportunities for wealth to hundreds of thousands of people across the globe than any form of business. Network marketing is the most excellent profession in today's free, capitalistic world without an upstart risk. But this does not make it a "get rich scheme."

To be successful in network marketing, you must take it seriously, make sacrifices, commit yourself, and be knowledgeable, the same way you will do in any other business.

The difference between it and the traditional business is that in network marketing, you reap the rewards to a higher level. To be knowledgeable in network marketing entails you being aware of the risks and of the problems you may face on the way, and therefore helping you stay a step ahead. You may be hardworking and dedicated to your endeavour, but are your efforts channeled towards the essential things? To assist you in ascertaining what you might be doing wrong, we will look at some mistakes to avoid if you must succeed in network marketing in this chapter:

Not Knowing Your Why

For every course you undertake in life, you should have an aim for doing it. Without a definite purpose for doing something, you may fall prey to the problems ahead in such venture. It is most vital in online network marketing.

Knowing your "why" will help you overcome any obstacles you encounter along the path to success as a professional network marketer.

Before venturing into the business, find out precisely your reason for joining the business. The stronger your "why", the farther you can go. Loss of interest and difficulty to continue will be comfortable without a strong basis for venturing into the business.

Unfortunately, many people get involved in the MLM movement without the slightest idea why.

People who are successful in network marketing put in great effort, time, energy, and concentration in building their organization.

No Basic Knowledge

Many people venture into an organization lacking proper understanding of the company and its management.

Without sufficient knowledge to what you are selling, you may lack the drive and motivation to sell it. It is essential to have motivation as the knowledge.

Previous experiences have hurt several individuals who led newbies to have a wrong view of the company as a whole. Ensure you do proper research on the company you consider venturing into. Don't allow yourself to get pressured into becoming a product or service distributor by someone who wants to sponsor you. If you don't care about being healthy, you probably won't sell a lot of health products. You must find something you are connected with and market those types of products.

To succeed in network marketing, consider the product. Health products are among the fastest selling products, so look into that line. Check out the financial backing of the company you intend joining. Do they have the aids of financial investors? It is an essential factor, and it is the primary reason for the failure of many MLM companies. It is very crucial to check the top management of the company, their background —

the length of time they have been involved in MLM. The level of success they have recorded. The company you intend joining should be young, progressive because this is where the opportunities exist. The earlier you get involved, the more chance you have of becoming wealthy.

Lack Of Self-Development

Absence of self-development in this business will present you as just another marketer doing the same thing. You need to sharpen your skills to stand out. It requires you to attend various conferences and significant events outside the planned activities of your company. Numerous articles are available on the internet, but it is crucial to mix up with renowned personalities who have been in the business for years, and this will alter your orientation about the company.

Meeting people of various cultures and background will significantly assist you in becoming successful. Equip yourself by regularly purchasing books and attending seminars.

Importantly, imagine yourself in a better situation than you are currently. Learn to train yourself.

Not Targeting The Right People

There is one area that network marketing companies need to get right – targeting the right people.

Once again, because this is relevant, especially for individuals in the online network marketing industry: not everyone is a potential prospect. The problem with not targeting the right people is that it can waste time and cause discouragement. Not everyone is a prospect. Avoid the mistake of trying to get anyone and everyone into your business. It is a fast way to separate and annoy people.

Traditionally, starting a business from scratch may require you to let your friends and family know about it, but smart business people identify their target market and pitch their business to them. Target a group of persons or market that is showing interest in the business rather than waste time and energy trying to get everyone involved.

A lot of successful network marketers have recruited friends and family, but the majority of their business partners is from people they didn't know initially. Also, most of the friends and family did not know until they saw the success of network marketing. It is easier. It also creates a lot of fun selling to individuals who are actively showing interest in what you have. You will also record more success.

Not Following Up

Follow up is to be done with people who have expressed interest in the product/service your business offers, and not wasted on those who have spelled it out that they are not interested. Many miss opportunities to develop their business by not following up on interested prospects.

While you are not expected to disturb people, most prospects aren't going to sign up on the first call. Sometimes, the timing may be wrong. Or they require some time to think about it and do their research. Develop a system for following up prospects.

For example, after a presentation and the individual is not ready, make an appointment to get in touch again in a few days. If they show no interest, ask if you can add them to your email list.

However, if people are adamant that they aren't interested, let it go. They may indicate interest once they see your success or maybe they never will. But ensure you don't hurt your relationships by continually trying to recruit people that are not interested.

Recruiting The Un-coachable

When in search of prospects to join your online network marketing business, the ability to come under a coach should be the first quality to look for, when you see that in an individual, you have located the right person.

The reason for getting someone you can coach is that if they're not willing to be coached, they will never follow the formula for network marketing as laid down by the company.

Having the required skills and talents is not sufficient; if they are not coachable, they are not a good match for you. Instead, they will waste your time and do as they wish and try reinventing the wheel. You may have little result from working with such a person in a network marketing business. If however, you find someone that is coachable and ready to work according to the system, work with them. Even if they don't start out having the required skills, they will learn.

Lack Of Team Spirit

If you lack team spirit, you should not expect to succeed in this business. The very essence of network marketing is to network amongst your team while working cohesively towards the same vision.

Network Marketing is an act that brings together a group of people for a mutual benefit. Having a team that you regularly communicate with helps you gain fresh ideas about the business and holds you accountable to the daily activities that will bring you closer to your desired goals.

Communicating with your organization helps you create the opportunity to inspire your team; and as well develop valuable and meaningful relationships with them.

To avoid falling victim of this common mistake, you could hold a weekly group meeting with your team and use the time to assess the performance of each other, give suggestions, provide feedback, and share insights on how to improve the overall performance of your group.

Disregarding Personal Development

Personal Development is an essential step that you must invest in to achieve success in building your mindset. Although you will be given various trainings, tools as well as mentors to guide you, your success relies on your ability to have the right mindset.

Personal Development is a highly encouraged practice and is necessary for every person who joins the business.

From business presentations to team meetings, you will discover that Personal Development is the basis for on which network marketing companies are built.

Disregarding this may cause failure in the business. If you haven't personally enforced it on yourself, then this might be the reason you are not on the path to success.

For you to progress, you have to learn the vital elements of personal development: technical knowledge, mindset, and leadership. You must keep in mind that personal development is a continuous process.

It doesn't stop in the four corners of schools and universities. So, always invest a great deal of your time feeding yourself with positive reinforcement and hang around successful and motivated people. The most successful in life and business know the importance of continuous learning. Continuing your education is essential when you are in network marketing. These are the skills that ensure you progress and become successful. The moment you decide to quit growing is the same moment you find that you have limited yourself and on what you can achieve in life.

Fear Of Failure

Risk is required when you want to succeed in life. People have been negatively affected by companies that made promises or by individuals who have assumed leadership positions and brought in new prospects into their company and at the end, no tangible result to show. But that is not enough reason to quit the company.

As difficult as it may appear, the network marketing business has changed a lot of persons with no skills, no primary education, and have taken them from rags to wealth.

Easily Affected By Rejection And Negative Outside Influence

Experiencing rejection directly from an individual that we least expect can be very difficult to bear. It does not only kill enthusiasm; it can also create self-doubt, especially for those just starting.

You may be unable to control what others say to you or their response towards you, but you can control how you respond to it. Be prepared; be optimistic every time, and train yourself to deal with rejection.

Remember, no one can steal your dreams without your permission.

Some allow problems to stop them in their path to success. Often, they have no significant reason for getting into network marketing in the first place, as this will determine how they will react to the obstacle. It is common for people to quit right before they begin to succeed.

Never give up. Build up and maintain a great support system around you. It may include team members as well as family and friends who are not involved in the business.

Magnify your "why" of the business. Recite positive affirmations each day to enable you to stay focused. When you make mistakes don't allow them to hinder you. Learn from them and keep moving ahead. Pardon yourself and remember that failure is not trying at all. With these in place, you are sure to succeed in network marketing.

Chapter 8: 25 Lessons Every Network Marketer Must Learn To Succeed

Network Marketing Requires Patience

I have been ruminating on those elements that separate the boys from men in this industry. What makes the difference between the movers and those who are static or passive?

Consistency is required to produce significant results. Prospecting is not a one-time affair; it should be done daily.

Now to the main point, I have discovered that many of us have been wired right from birth to fail. We expect things to turn out right overnight. Microwave ovens, lotteries, fast food provide instant gratification. We are programmed the same way to earn our daily living. We work monthly, and we earn a salary.

The reverse is the case in Network Marketing; things do not occur very fast. Immediately you join a network marketing company; you start combating this default setting of get-rich-quick. Patience is the key ingredient to build a long-lasting business.

Tips On Patience

- Do not compare your results or success with others.
- Be aware that it takes time to succeed.
- See network marketing as your business and not a salary job. It takes time for business to grow. Imagine if your boss never built his or her business, you would not have been part of the success story.
- If you are wondering why you are not achieving quick results in your network marketing business, then take these two approaches - fight your default programming, or accept the reality that it takes time to build a successful business.
- Network Marketing's demand will test your attitude no matter where you start from and what you start with

I have met different individuals struggling with their MLM businesses. Some of them lament how things were not working according to what they planned, and how they were not making the money they were once excited about when they attended the prospect meeting.

When they ask me these questions, they are always expecting me to give them a magic wand on how to make the business work. I always tell them that they are the biggest problem with the Network Marketing business. A negative attitude is one of the most challenging limitations in the network marketing business. If you cultivate the right attitude in this business, you will become successful.

These attitude adjustments will help you achieve success in your network marketing business.

Focus

You cannot achieve significant strides if you do not keep your eyes on your goals. If you join the business based on how you feel or when things are going smoothly, you may not attain success. Network Marketing demands consistency and focus. Have a goal that you are always working towards.

Personal Development

You can only achieve what you have become. Network Marketing demands constant honing of your skills. You need to read books on MLM, watch videos of industry experts, and attend seminars and workshops. Have this mindset of always wanting to learn something new if you want to succeed.

Time Consciousness

If you want to earn good passive and residual income, you will need to become generous with your time and knowledge. What this means is to train your team and network continually; keep in touch with them and answer every question relating to the business. Whatever you give will always come back to you.

Self-Confidence

Self-confidence is not pride. It does not also mean you have to be cocky. But if you don't believe in yourself, nobody will believe in you. They can easily know when you lack confidence. This is the reason you need to present yourself with confidence.

A positive attitude will help you succeed in this business. If you exhibit negative energy, then failure is inevitable. You will succeed!

Diligence And Commitment Are Needed To Succeed In Network Marketing

What is Diligence?

It is the constant and consistent effort to accomplish your objectives and goals; exerting your body and mind without procrastination, unnecessary delay. A diligent network marketer is focused, action-oriented, consistent, careful, attentive, and productive. He is bound to be successful against all the odds.

Commitment is being faithful to a course or loyal to someone (up-line, superior/line manager), or something (organization) and practicing loyalty consistently irrespective of contrary situations.

Some essentials point to implement to qualify for loyalty:

- Protect the interest of your organization
- Say good things about your MLM business
- Defend your business even if it will cost you
- Show commitment to selling your company products
- Dedicate time to build your business
- Pray for the success of your MLM organization and team
- Go the extra mile
- Trust the judgment of your up-line.

There are people to meet in Network Marketing, and there are people to miss. Don't hold on to friends you are meant to let go.

Here are 11 steps to manage your friends in Network Marketing

- Keep a low expectation. Don't focus on getting them out of business. It seems they have become impediments to the growth of your business, reduce your expectations from them so your dream can grow.

- Understand you are in the business for the long term. It will take more than a single chat or conversation to make them believe in your dream.

- Do not make them look stupid and act like you are better and smarter.

- Know your foes! Know your friends.

- Be true to yourself, even if close relatives pull out.

- Realize that people are bound to change. Never relate with people based on what they used to be, but what they are now.

- Do not talk down on other people's MLM.

- Don't buy their MLM products or be a part of their team. Why? It simply means you support their unethical business model, and you will likely replicate the same tactics they use to draw you into the business.

- Maintain a distant relationship from friends participating in other MLM business. This will make them come to you when they need your support.
- Share your life experience with your friends before you start your Network Marketing Business.
- Share other aspects of your life from different perspectives. Instead of talking about the business, talk about the kids.

No One Can Succeed Alone In Network Marketing; You Need Mentors And A Strong Team

Successful leaders in Network Marketing possess the ability to surround themselves with fellow proficient leaders and MLM business owners. Your network, they say, determines your net worth. You cannot rise above the level of your network. That's why it is essential to be part of a great team and also subscribe for mentorship.

Network Marketing depends on a team of individuals working together to accomplish team success. TEAM means Together Each Achieves Much. Each member is required to embrace the common vision and goals for the business to succeed. If you are planning to join a network marketing business, you are about to unravel the significance of up-lines and down-lines.

The most successful networker in the world is the one who adopts a bottom-up strategy. You can be successful by replicating the achievements of others in this business.

In the bottom-up strategy, every team member contributes his or her quota to the actualization of the common goal. The best MLM business focuses on leadership development. Focus is directed at growing leaders that perfectly understand the business and can educate others. Those leaders are also capable of developing exceptional teams and affiliates to promote the business and assist network affiliates in improving.

A lot of up-line leaders have adopted the top-down strategy and recorded significant setback as they fail to leverage on the potentialities of their down-lines. They are managing down-lines instead of leading them to build a sustainable business.

As a Network Marketer who desires to be successful, collaborating with a leader or business that utilizes a bottom-up approach is essential. These MLM organizations provide duplicable models easily and mentoring programs to assist down-line. As a leader builds his or her team and increases in the knowledge of the industry and the business, the capacity to train down-lines and recruits is enhanced, and this goes a long way to optimize the overall performance of the team.

Give Your Best When You Have The Opportunity

A well-utilized opportunity can boost your Network Marketing business forever

Here are three tips to maximizing every opportunity in your Network Marketing Business:

- **Create Goals That Exceed Your Target**

  Examine the industry leaders and top achievers and increase your expectations or targets ten times of what they have accomplished. Then establish a plan based on this lofty goal. For instance, if the top achievers were earning $60,000 a year, create a plan on how you can make $600,000 yearly. That sounds absurd and crazy! Yes, it is. You may not meet your target, but you will inevitably end up in the 1% of top achievers in the industry.

- **Develop A 'Why' To Keep You Going**

  Network Marketers and a lot of business owners often miss a purpose to keep them inspired in the pursuit of their objectives. It is not enough to set targets; you must arm yourself with the reasons to keep working in this industry. You can use an aggressive time management planning, for instance.

- **Ensure You Are Sold First**

  The most significant sale you will ever make in this business is the one you sell to yourself. For instance, you can cold call your team members and gather their testimonies and success stories. This will help you to be deeply committed to helping people. Then, create a list of prospects who will need your products and services and devise the means of reaching them. High achieving networkers understand prospects do not just appear. They always stay on the aggressive hunt to enrich their pipeline.

- **The Power Of Duplication**

  It is legal to copy and know how to paste. Successful networkers have learned how to copy and replicate what has worked for others. This includes best practices in network marketing.

"It does not matter what works; duplication is the key."

Duplication is as old as Network Marketing. It is the foundation on which Network Marketing is built. It does not matter the skills and strategies that work for you; if they are not duplicable for your down-lines, you are not going to succeed in this business. Recruiting is not enough; there is a need to teach your new prospects what you do, how you do it, and why they need to do it. However, you should understand that the fact that something works for you does not mean it will produce the same results for others. For instance, if your strategy is to talk to celebrities, it may not work for your new down-lines. It is always problematic when network marketing leaders get excited about what works for them and fail to build systems in their organizations on how to replicate the same. The bottom line is to create a simplified system that can be duplicated by any dummy in your organization.

Testimonies And Proofs Will Sell Better Than Mere Words Of Mouth

Every MLM business aspires to provide time and money freedom for people. How do you convince them to join if you cannot prove that with testimonies?

Nevertheless, no one will want to join you because he or she does not like time and money freedom. Everyone wants to get out of debt and have more time to spend with their loved ones. Now, if they all desired time and money freedom. What's stopping them from joining us in this business? Proof!

People will not believe it until they see proofs. Instead of talking to them about the benefits, share how it has transformed the lives of your up-line if you don't have a personal testimony yet.

Appreciate Individual Differences

To be a successful network marketing leader, four essential traits are needed. Develop these characteristics, and you will be glad you did.

- **Vitality**

    Another word for this is high energy or being dominant. It simply means to be courageous. It is a major trait of every successful networker who has conquered limiting beliefs.

    By choosing this profession, you have signed up for a major shift in your life. You have to appreciate the importance of vitality. Vitality is a spirit and it is very contagious. It revolves around every aspect of life-physical, financial, spiritual and relational. If you possess vitality, let others know about it. Make it known by what you wear, how you smile, and what you eat.

- **Authenticity**

    Be real! Be you! Be honest!

Don't pretend to be who you are not. You will be remembered for what you do, not what you say you will do. There is no shortcut in this industry. Every significant change begins with you and emanates from within. If people discover you are living a fake life, they will turn their back on you.

Once you have become successful, you will understand that who you have become is more valuable than what you have accomplished.

- **Loyalty**

    Loyalty means having an enthusiastic commitment to an important relationship that will impact you in the long haul. People follow leaders. If you change business, you will likely have a lot of people that will follow you. People would rather stick to someone they trust even if the business model does not make sense.

- **Receptiveness**

It means openness. I don't prospect someone that is not open. It is a sheer waste of time. I always ask, "Are you open to a new direction?" Network Marketing is about openness. Going into the world with your eyes opened and your ears ready to hear an opportunity that transforms lives.

Focus On Your Strength And Not Your Weaknesses

Focus produces clarity of vision. Strength is what you can do and what turns you on while weakness is what you can delegate and turns you off. While impossibility should not be in your dictionary, there are things others can do better than you. Goats cannot hunt like cats at night. An eagle cannot swim like a fish in the ocean.

How Can You Focus?

- Define your goals and objectives
- Create a map or game plan to accomplish them
- Plan your time

- Do the first thing first
- Ignore the noise to make the news
- Don't procrastinate
- Be accountable

Be Disciplined To Succeed In Network Marketing

Achievers in network marketing exhibit a high level of self-control. Don't engage in activities that are detrimental to your relationship with God, your family, and yourself. Self-Discipline is learned; we are not born with it.

The truth is that anyone can become a network marketer if you possess the needed skills, knowledge and understanding of the business, the money to buy the starter kits to start your business and communication skills, but all these skills and knowledge will amount to so little or worse, nothing if you lack the discipline to manage those qualities and run a good business.

Discipline is a very valuable quality that anyone who desires to achieve success in network marketing must cultivate in order to grow their business to the level they desire.

Discipline means that you manage your time effectively and do away with things and events that distract you from achieving your desired target. Discipline is not a quality we inherit or born with, but an attribute that we learn and master. It is the ability to develop habits that leads to a better and productive work ethic. You need be disciplined to be successful in the Network Marketing business or you fail.

Apply Wisdom

There is wisdom you will never get until the need arises in your Network Marketing business. Every situation will present a problem that only you can solve. How you solve it is dependent on the people you have met and the books you have read.

The best form of wisdom comes from learning from your mistakes, turning your failures and rejections into stepping stones that will propel you to achieve the success you desire. Another way you can learn the wisdom to apply in your business is through learning from your mentors/sponsors, reading books on network marketing, listening to tapes and attending seminars.

Respect Those Who Have Gone Ahead

You cannot contact grace that you don't honor. You must respect those who have gone ahead of you no matter their age in the Network Marketing business. If you want to learn the wisdom of the elders, you must honor the elders. Honor those who have spent time to make this industry reputable. You can do this by reading their books and attending their seminars when they visit town.

Age Is Inconsequential In Network Marketing

You are not too small to be great! Anybody who desires greatness in life can have it. Age is not important. You can be the oldest and be great, and you can be the youngest and succeed as well. Do not look down on yourself.

You are not too young to become the next success story in network marketing, or too old to become a part of the network marketing family. All that you need is the motivation, passion and determination to succeed.

Overtaking Is Possible

No position is ever permanent in the Network Marketing business; that means, your down-lines can make more money than you.

The hand of the diligent makes productive. If you are diligent and consistent, you can be what you want to be. Don't be intimidated by the success of others; strive to achieve significance as well.

Competition Is The Fuel For Growth

The world would be static if there were no competition. Millions of sperm cells compete but only one becomes a baby; likewise, nations compete and one emerges the World Cup Champion. The prize is reserved for those who can outperform others. If the Lion fails to compete in the forest, he will die a Lion King.

What's The Bottom Line?

Do not rest on your oars and watch things happen; rise to make things happen. Competition is real in the Network Marketing business. Up your game to stay in the game. Everyone is fishing in the same pool, so raise your game to beat the competition!

Integrity Is Cash

Network Marketing is about honesty. If the product does not work, it will not move. Never prioritize anything above integrity in the Network Marketing business. A lot of people will exchange their integrity for money; such people will never go far in this business.

For instance, a down-line invites you to train his or her prospects; you then go behind him/her and sign those prospects up without his/her knowledge. I see a lot of people do this in Network

Marketing. Your growth is a function of your integrity.

Avoid Scam And Get Rich Quick

A lot of get-rich-quick businesses have come and gone. They don't last. It takes time to build anything good. Don't invest your time and money in scam and schemes that promise bring N50, 000 to earn N100, 000. It may cost you money, time, and relationships. What you lose will be more than the promised gains.

Establish Structures

Teamwork is one of the stable structures that can make you build a reliable business. Focus on the structure before incentives. Once the structure is solid, it will naturally produce. Invest in your team. Train them consistently; once they are trained, they will replicate your results.

Be Confidential

It is not everything you see that you say. This goes against the familiar slogan, "See something, say something." The only person that deserves your secret is a wise listener.

Make Your Team Active

Ensure that most of your teammates are active and be aware that every year, you will lose important people in your Network Marketing business to a new opportunity. The only constant thing is change.

Recruit The Best

Do you know companies recruit and don't employ everyone? It is not everyone you prospect that you recruit. It does not matter if they have the money to join. Work smart to recruit some good fishes into your net always.

Develop Yourself

Grow fast if you want to make an impact in Network Marketing. Equipping yourself is to your credit. Apply KEY – Keep Educating Yourself. This is very essential for your success.

Care For Your Team

Caring for your team is very important. Be a welfarist. It will make your Network Marketing business grow fast.

Be Humble

Humility will elevate you when others think you don't qualify. BE HUMBLE, STAY HUMBLE!

Chapter 9: The Potentials In Network Marketing (Aims Global As A Model)

The potential of network marketing as a business is very promising, and that makes it the business of choice for anyone aspiring to grow a big and successful business.

In the past ten years, network marketing has been the business with the highest growth rate. In a period of ten years, network marketing recorded an annual revenue selling increase of 7.1%, higher than the economy growth of most economically viable countries in the world.

AIM Global, otherwise known as Alliance in Motion Global, has been one of the network marketing companies that have experienced tremendous growth and success since the inception of the company, and this growth and success is not being enjoyed by the company alone, but also by all its affiliates.

From the inception of AIM Global in 2015, the company has put the interest, growth and success of its distributors at the forefront. This pro-distributor mindset has made the company one of the fastest growing network marketing companies with an estimated membership of 6 million people, with presence in the fastest growing continents in the world.

The truth is that any business model that has achieved the level of success achieved by network marketing should be emulated, learnt from and embraced.

AIMS Global as a network marketing company is designed with the growth and success of its distributors in mind. Their unique system and ways of operation has enabled their distributors to grow their business beyond their dreams.

Some of the things that make the company unique and the company of choice for any success oriented distributor are:

- AIM Global is the first and the only network marketing company that gives payouts daily to its distributors, and this daily payouts have been going on for 12 years now, and this is something that no other network marketing company has achieved.

- Some of the countries benefitting from this daily payouts includes: Philippines, Nigeria, Rwanda, Togo, Papua New Guinea, Uganda, UAE, Ghana, Cameroon, Kenya, Pakistan, Kenya, Tanzania and Ivory Coast.

- This great feat has not gone unnoticed, and that is why in 2018, AIM Global received an international innovative award for being the first network marketing company to effectively implement the daily payouts system.

- AIMS Global has invested massively in the IT infrastructure which makes it very easy and convenient for the company's distributors to monitor the performance of their sales online, anywhere in the world and even while relaxing comfortably in their homes.

- This innovative infrastructure breakthrough eliminates the stress the distributors would have gone through in going to company's offices to check their income and commission. The system works 24/7, and it is user friendly and secure.

- The type of products that a company offers is one of the factors that determines its growth and success and that of the distributors; AIM Global is one of the best network marketing companies that offers quality and value driven products.

- AIM Global is the sole maker of Nature's way products, a reputable and well known company that produces high quality health and wellness products, and over a period of over 36 years, the partners to AIM Global (Nature's Way) have taken herbal and nutritional science to an unprecedented level.

Nature's way is well known in America as the number one company that produces dietary and nutritional supplements. Some of the things that make Nature's Way products exceptional and AIM Global an ideal networking company to join in network marketing business include:

- The very first herbal and nutritional supplement producer that has a licensed state of the art production facility.
- The first organic products producer to receive a certification.
- The first herbal and nutritional supplement company to introduce plant based medicine (Phyto-medicine) into the market.
- The first company to protect health freedom and spent millions of dollars doing so.
- The first company to fund other companies to propagate health information and ensure quality.

There is a lot of firsts for Nature's Way and AIM Global is an integral part of these success stories. And that is why AIM Global is one of the best network marketing companies that guarantees success for its distributors and provide a lot of potentials for growth and development.

AIM Global is more than a business. It is a family of network marketers and committed business owners working together to ensure the growth and success of the company and its over 6 million members in many countries in the world.

Chapter 10: What You Must Do To Be An Achiever

Being an achiever is the desire of virtually every human being on earth. The desire to become an achiever is so strong that many pursue it the passionately, not minding the cost.

Unfortunately, the hope of many to become an achiever is unguided as they lack the know-how to actually become an achiever.

Achievers are those who have a great deal of self-motivation, work smart not necessarily hard, and have dogged determination and dedication to accomplish their dream.

They usually are driven by results. They set goals and targets and would not allow anything to come between them and the achievement of those set goals and objectives.

The belief that achievers are endowed with resources (human, financial and material) is faulty and based on assumptions as the success stories of most of the achievers in the world shows the otherwise.

The right question to ask then is 'who is an achiever?' An achiever is a reasonable person in the ordinary world that sees and approaches life issues from different and extraordinary angles. He or she is a person that is not afraid of failing; hence, never takes "no" for an answer but keeps failing until the result is achieved. An achiever sees failure, not as an end in itself, but a means to the expected end - success.

An achiever expects challenges in life and rises to the task to surmount the obstacles as they know that challenges are an opportunity to succeed and not a stumbling block to success. Impossibility does not exist in the dictionary of an achiever; instead, every problem is a trial for the next phase in life.

The significant difference between an achiever and the ordinary person in life is their mentality.

A mindset is a thought pattern, a belief system. A mindset determines how one approach issues of life and perspective in life. The mindset of an achiever includes a burning desire for success, goal-setting and goal-getting, a full understanding and deployment of self to attain success, one that takes full responsibilities for their actions, goals and life in general, amongst many others.

Achievers are not born so; they decided to make a difference with their lives, committed to same and became their desires. They necessarily do not set out with the motive of solely being achievers. They are just people committed to meeting every little target they set for themselves; they form a habit of success and end up being great. The pattern formed makes everything they touch or set out to achieve turn excellent; making them appears as though they have a magic wand to do things.

On the contrary, they are people committed to excellence with nothing enough to curb them from achieving success.

You can be an achiever also. You have everything it takes to become all that you desire to be. You are equipped, fortified, and destined to achieve your goals. You are not meant to be a mission that cannot be achieved; you are a mission that will be achieved. You are more than what you think yourself to be. You are great and extraordinary. You are meant for the very top in your world and your chosen path in life. You are the true definition of success. Your world awaits your greatness; shine on! Do you wonder who I am talking about? I am talking about you!

You are shocked to the bone that you can be described as I have done. You do not have to be so surprised. The problem is you don't believe any good thing can be attached to you needless to talk of you being good.

You have a limiting mindset and low opinion of yourself, such that any little affliction on your road to success seems to be too much for you to handle. In as much as I mean no disrespect, I intend to get that limiting mentality out of you and the only way to achieve that is to face it.

Many people have said a lot of things to you that have negatively affected your self-esteem and self-belief. No more!

You are being restored to your original state and place in life; first in your mindset (thinking) then in life. You are made to be a difference in your world. You are created uniquely and as a solution to your world. You cannot allow the negative comments and opinions of mediocre sway you from becoming all you are configured to be by your Maker. You are wired to be an achiever naturally. You will become one by committing to the principles shared in this chapter and the whole book. Are you ready to become an achiever you are meant to be? Then, let's examine the principles guiding the life and living of achievers.

Be Proactive

Achievers are not reactionary people, they are proactive. They do not react to issues and events of life.

Life is best lived prepared for. There are many things that would not happen in your life until you deliberately cause them to happen. You have to be prepared for every good and bad turn in life. The major way achievers prepare for life is reading books they can glean valuable lessons from.

I remember two events I experienced some years back that is worth mentioning here.

One, a senior communal brother saw me with a book titled 'Why A students work for C students, and B students work for the government' by Robert Kiyosaki and commented on passing. He said, 'why do you enjoy wasting your money on books that add no value to your life? Why don't you rather buy something you can enjoy with your money; things like food and drinks?' My answer shut him up for life, I said: 'Would you rather waste about 50 years of experience the author packed in the book or use a few thousands of Naira (the Nigeria currency) to buy the about 50 years of experience?' he got my message as he could not answer me a word.

Secondly, many years ago, when I camped for 21 days to undergo the compulsory government-organized one-year youth service program (NYSC), I invested my money in buying 28 books. I was buying one today and the other tomorrow, and keeping the books with a vendor. A day to our departure from camp, I went to carry my newly acquired assets and was shocked at the response of my colleagues. The vocal one amongst them said, 'Do you want to become a book vendor? Or why would you buy these much books?' My simple response is that 'Readers are Leaders.' What amazed me the most of the second occurrence is the fact that I motivated my colleagues to be readers as I was and still am, but the reaction I got from them clearly showed why Nigerian youths are not leading the nation yet.

Reading prepares you for the future as it exposes the mind to information and lessons from experiences of others that are worth learning from. Or would you rather go the hard way of learning from your experience when there is someone that has gone through the same and is generous enough to write it in a book.

Grabbing the book and reading the same is wisdom. Reading extensively fortifies the mind with information that would be called upon when situations of life raise their heads — reading arms one through life. You become armed in life that can no longer be harmed. Reading is an advantage in life. While it should be emphasized that reading is beyond the walls of a classroom or an institution, it must be done with the right motive and purpose at heart.

Like reading, attending seminars, talks, conferences, etc. have a similar advantage as reading just that they add visuals, sound, commentaries, and varying opinions to what have been written.

When you become proactive, you are a step ahead of others in becoming your true self and achieving your set targets in life. As the motto of the Boys Scout Association in Nigeria goes, BE PREPARED.

Live Intentional

Without being intentional about living, life becomes aimless, and whatever comes is accepted as the best. When nothing is expected, anything and everything that happens in life is accepted. To become an achiever, there must be a deliberate attempt to become an achiever, and also, there must be a deliberate attempt at being an achiever at something specifically.

You are endowed in some areas of life. What some struggle to achieve, you can achieve it without breaking a sweat. You are a solution provider to some problems and issues in life, and you do the same effortlessly and swiftly. Everything you do without struggle is an indication of what you are created for. You must be purposeful about your skillset popularly referred to as **PURPOSE** or **DREAMS**.

Your purpose is the reason for your existence. You owe yourself the responsibility of fulfilling your dreams. Your achievement in life is directly proportional to the fulfillment of your dream. Do you want to be an achiever? Achieve your dreams! Your dreams are the wings on which your life would fly high. Do not damage your life by clipping your dreams. Go for gold; live your dreams.

Achievers are deliberate about achieving their dreams. They are fully aware of the fact that their dreams are all their life is about. Hence, they live deliberately and carefully about the dream.

They discover their dreams, develop it, and deploy the same to achieve maximum returns. Being that it is only wise to copy a winning formula, you must discover your dreams (simplified into your skillsets), develop the dreams (by reading, attending seminars, and meeting people of like minds), and deploy the dreams to the world to yield maximum returns; impacting the world.

The mistake many make while deploying their dreams is the greedy desire for financial returns. In as much as financial returns would grace the deployment of the dreams, the motive of deployment must always be impacting the world. When your dreams catch the heart of your world, it naturally catches their pocket for where the heart of a man is, his resources flow and follow.

Live deliberately to achieve your dreams; setting distractions aside and focusing on your focus. You would only become an achiever once you achieve your dreams. The only way to achieve your dreams is to work on your dreams. Are you ready? Work out your dreams as your world awaits your impending manifestation.

Associate With Achievers

The companies you keep either make or mar you. You are defined by the five closest people to you. Who you are is visibly defined by those in your circle of influence.

You cannot rise beyond your company. Choose your company wisely. Choose your company with your dreams in sight. Just as the saying, 'birds of like feather flock together' goes; your association determines the height you attain in life.

Achievers are more deliberate about those they allow into their lives as they know the importance of people being in their lives. Positive people go in the direction of their dreams and their set targets and goals.

Negative people, on the other hand, are people that help you waste your life. They have no mission in life and would ensure that you have no purpose. They are distractions to living as they live only for the immediate without any sight of a better tomorrow. To negative people, today is the end; tomorrow is not essential.

You must do all you can to avoid association with negative people. They will sap you of your strength for your dream, rob you of your dreams, and ensure you live an aimless, purposeless life. You are better off with no company at all than with negative people. Do yourself a favor by being around great minds.

Have you forgotten so soon the cliché throw around of small people discussing people and great people discussing ideas? This cliché should be the sieve you use to filter people in life. Those that come to you to consider someone will go to the other person to talk about you; you don't need them in your life. You need people who come to you with excellent and bright ideas on how to achieve your dreams and set goals. These are people working their dreams and want you to work yours to ensure the world is a better place.

These people believe that there are too many opportunities to be explored than only they can hence seek the company of world changers that would join in living the dreams and making a world a better place.

Life is not like a bed of roses without thorns. You should not expect a great association without a price. The cost required of you is living your dreams. Once you set out living your dreams, life would orchestrate the right association you need to attain the height of your dreams. The right company would demand from you, and shape you to the achiever you are destined to be. You would be as high as your dreams when you pursue your dreams with the right company. Build a great company, and your goals would birth to multiple companies.

Be Value Focused

Nothing cripples the destiny of a young more than misplaced priorities. Intent and motive must be right before the result is right. The purpose of doing a thing is like the foundation of a building.

If the foundation is not right from the beginning, the edifice built on it will come crumbling no matter the height of it. The motive is the foundation of your dreams. To what end is the goal you desire to achieve?

Achievers know from the very beginning of living their dream that the intention of birthing the dream is to impact the world for good and make it a better place to live. They set out in pursuit of adding value to their world. With the genuineness of the motive of creating and adding value to the world, they become valuable themselves, and since value attracts value, value chases after them.

Just as no one moves forward looking back, value creation must be your focus if you truly want to become an achiever in life. The world recognizes value when it sees one. Make your life about creating value and focus solely on the same to achieve a valuable life and become valuable. Your focus must be on values you can add to your world at every point in time. The world achievers we celebrate today are people that saw the world as missing some things, and rather than complain about the problem, they set themselves to become a lasting solution to them. Hence they become great achievers.

What are the problems you had seen as problems before? You need to have a change in perspective and see them, not merely as problems, but as opportunities waiting to be harnessed, and as platforms, you can leverage on to become the achiever you desire. There is no other secret to success than seeing challenges as opportunities and harnessing the same to your advantage. As you do so, your focus must be value addition other than monetary value to be amassed.

Life is too short to live solely for returns. A life lived for creating value, and adding value to the world is one well lived and would be one whose name would be engraved in the sands of time. A good name, they say, is far better than rubies. Pursue after a good name, and rubies you desire would naturally flow in your direction.

Have Routines

The secret of success that achievers found out is that success is in repetition. Achievers do the same thing over and again consistently without getting tired or losing focus. Why? They know that in doing that lays the power of achievement.

Being repetitive is tasking and tedious; it takes a committed person to keep that up. There are necessary actions that get an achiever the results he or she has today. To produce the same results, the same steps must be taken.

More fundamentally, achievers have a prescriptive way of living. Every second is valuable to them, and they do not joke with their time. Time to an achiever is more than money; time is life. There is a dotted line between what is to be done now and the next. They place tremendous value on their time, such that time wasters have no place near them.

Or have you not noticed that an ordinary person would instead save money and spend time while an achiever would spend money and save time?

Let me paint a scenario to clarify better this:

An ordinary person would have an appointment in a distant place, say on a Monday, and would prefer to be in the place or a nearby location since Saturday or Sunday to arrive at the location of the appointment early on the appointed day. An achiever, on the other hand, has such a busy routine that he cannot afford such luxury of time to waste hence concentrates on his or her methods and boards a plane to the location of the appointment on the appointed day to return the same day.

What did you deduce? What an achiever does for his or her world is more important than what the world pushes to him or her. That further buttresses the fact of being deliberate with their approach to life and living, being focused on value creation and addition, being proactive and associating with like-minded people.

There is a mentality achievers have that generates the kind of life they live.

It is the mentality of an achiever that makes the difference; little wonder they carefully choose their association to avoid contamination. You can be the achiever you are meant to be. You can impact your world even better than some achievers we celebrate today. Once you commit to the principles of an achiever and the new mind-set to replace the old in you, you are on the pathway of becoming your desires.

Scripted Living

Living for an achiever is beyond mere wishful thinking. Living is according to a script the Maker made them with. An achiever seeks to act the text of his or her life. There is a traditional way of life once you set out to become an achiever. Your life is no longer yours but the world's. You are no longer a private or personal being. You are now a public image proffering solutions to the problems and challenges of the world.

Because of the script being lived by, achievers always have a script around and about them detailing what to do and sometimes how to do it. Achievers do not live on wishful thinking; instead; they are deliberate and detailed about living that they commit mostly all they do to writing. They maintain an organized to-do list and follow through with the dictates of the to-do list.

When an achiever's life is assessed, they tend to appear as organized and perfect to the world. They tend to lead a seamless and error-free life. But what most people do not know about them is that their errors and working are first done on paper, while they subsequently act the script. Is it any wonder that they are proactive and appear to achieve results without breaking much sweat? Since a large part of this session seems repetitive; the principles of being an achiever are repetitive and intertwined. It will be a huge mistake if this write-up follows another direction than being repetitive.

You must understand that there is a script about you made by your Maker. You must discover the script and live in consonance with it, and also create your script to live in agreement with the divine script. You must live by the books; your to-do list would go a long way in helping you organize your thoughts and your life. Script your life; engage a to-do list.

Self-Discipline

Self-discipline is deliberately left as the last principle of becoming an achiever because of the weight it carries in the principles. The hardest person to lead in the world is self. It is easier to command and direct others on what to do and what not to do, but it is tough to lead self in a course. Self-discipline is the most important of all the principles of becoming an achiever.

Achievers neither loiter around nor waste away their lives. They have a handle on themselves that they can control both their desires and their appetite for everything. This makes them control themselves and their activities to point the same in the direction of the goals they set out to achieve.

Self-discipline is best explained as critically considering the effects of any action or inaction without any sense of sentiment or prejudice. It is the imposition of a limit on yourself to ensure that you achieve the set goals as against self-aggrandizement. It is the essential principle in the making of an achiever.

If you can lead yourself, you can become an achiever. Once a person is out of the way of achieving the dreams, the dream becomes more explicit, and achievement of the same becomes easier as focus shifts from self to the dream.

With self-discipline, there is a huge play down on self alone and an accommodation of other possible options and alternatives to achieve the dreams.

Have you not noticed the ploy of achievers in the world? Most of them do not own any of the resources used in impacting the world, save the idea and the leadership to achieving the dreams. They use other people's resources (time, money and skill) to deliver their course. They master the art and craft of limiting themselves and allowing others to take center stage in the achievement of their goals. Isn't that rather funny?

Self-discipline embeds all the other principles and sieves them. You accommodate the pivotal ones and discard the irrelevant ones. With self-discipline in place, an achiever is undoubtedly made. Do you genuinely desire yourself an achiever? Discipline yourself to become one.

Conclusion

It has been recognized that desires are lame though achievable. The pursuit of the desires make the desires see the light of the day. The principles discussed in the pages of this book are the major pursuit you need to see your desires become a reality. But the quest is the work; you must be ready to commit to the working of the principles if you want see your desire of being an achiever materialize.

Aside pursuit, your mentality must be that of an achiever; not seeking after gains for what you do, but seeking impact.

Impacting the world must be your focus, and once your impact grips the heart of your world, your world would yield up the value or gains you want. Do not misplace your priorities; impact your world, and see your world impact your life with values.

Do not sit complaining about challenges and problems. They are not obstacles to your life but are stepping stones to the attainment of your dreams. See challenges as opportunities for you to impact your world for good. Achievers see challenges as opportunities; do the same. Problems come your way to lift you, not to curb your progress. That's the mind-set!

Your world is ready for the reality of your dreams. Your world is prepared to have you as an achiever impacting it for good. Are you ready?

Overview

In a network marketing arrangement, individuals relate with a parent organization as a franchisee or an independent contractor and are paid based on their sales accrued by those they introduce into the business. This can be compared to franchise frameworks where royalties are compensated from the sales of individual franchise activity to the franchiser as well as to a regional or area manager.

In a legitimate Network or Multi-Level Marketing Company, commissions accrue only on sales of the organization's products and services. You cannot earn from sign-up fees. It is ideal for analyzing the compensation plan to know whether recruits are paid from sales or sign-up fees. If compensation is from money received from those who join the business, then the company is a Ponzi scheme or an illegal pyramid scheme.

Some less legal organizations generate revenues primarily by recruiting new people with the expectation of reward and selling products or services with no value or dubious value at an exorbitant price. This is against selling products consumers will purchase with no strings attached.

There is a need to evaluate the products or services and know the significant portion of clients that would buy them if they do not make money from the attached opportunity. If the product or service has no value or dubious value, or if recruits must buy excessive quantities without a conscious intention to utilize or resell them, then the company is a discreetly veiled pyramid scheme.

Network Marketing is simple, and we do it every day. We recommend our family and friends to the barbershops, restaurants, religious organizations, telecommunication services, boutiques, and the list is endless. We don't get paid for doing those activities. Network marketing aspires to reward you for sharing the good news with your friends and families. If the product is excellent, you will generously tell others about it.

I hope you have learned some valuable truth by coming across this book. If you find this book resourceful, you can recommend it to your friends and families too.

THE AUTHOR

Wale Oyeniyi is a man of many parts. He is a Teacher, a gifted Author, a Preacher, an Educationist, a Philanthropist, and an Entrepreneur.

An Alumnus of Obafemi Awolowo University (OAU), The Redeemed Christian Church of God Bible College and Haggai Institute, USA. He has attended several leadership courses at home and abroad.

He is a friend and mentor to many people around the world. He is an adherent proponent of leadership by example. He is much sought after as a speaker in churches, seminars, and conferences

He is the President of RightFinder© International, an NGO that amongst other things specialize in organizing seminars, conferences, prayer meetings, counseling, educating Youths, Young Adults, and leaders of businesses and ministers of the Gospel around the world.

He is happily married and enjoying God's best with his family.

NOTES

www.ingramcontent.com/pod-product-compliance
Lightning Source LLC
Chambersburg PA
CBHW021357210526
45463CB00001B/126